About This Book

One Dog And His Man is a comme
the human race and its eccentricities th
Labrador of uncommon perception ca
illustrated by the late cartoonist, Larry.

Each chapter reveals a new insight into a different aspect
of life seen through the wickerwork of the dog basket and
uncovers those tricks that our canine chums use to make their
own life simpler and ours more confusing.

From sound advice on food of all kinds and tips on
acquiring it from the passer by to observations on the mating
rituals of the human male, One Dog And His Man tackles a
wide range of inter species minefields such as human
offspring, seasonal variations, training and even the media.

This is an essential work for any dog wishing to make
sense of the people around him.

© Mike Henley, 2012
Illustrations by Larry © 2012

ISBN 978-1-4716-6035-1

Chapter 1 On Misery

You simply would not believe what I have to put up with. First there was the lawn. For no good reason, the Boss suddenly decided that life would not be worth living unless he had a lawn at the back of the house, in between a selection of misshapen grey concrete slabs he refers to as 'the patio' and a low brick wall where you can do yourself a lot of damage whilst in hot pursuit of that irritating ex tomcat from Number 36.

A lawn - I ask you! The patch under discussion has, for as long as I can remember, housed a restful collection of butterflies and bees and other fauna all happily plying their various trades. You'll find the occasional rusty trowel, perhaps a handful of empty wine bottles still bearing a heady trace of their former contents, that old rowing machine he bought on a whim in a completely unsuccessful attempt to regain his lost vigour. Nothing outrageous, you understand, but worth a sniffy stroll around when he's too tired to take me for a wander or too dignified for a tussle on the rug in front of the fire.

Mind you, I should have recognised the symptoms. Off and on for nearly three weeks he would gaze out of the kitchen window, hands clasped behind his back. A grunt. A sigh. Then, 'I really must do something about that.' Now under normal circumstances such a total lack of positive intent would barely cause a chap to raise the old snout above feed bowl level. Not the sort of Statement of Objectives that would prompt you to say, 'stand by with the grass seed, there's action afoot.' No. Of course I ignored him, always the safest way when he's in one of his musing moods. At his most distant he's even capable of stroking me against the grain which is so annoying. Keep your head down, Oberon old chap, I thought to myself, the mood will pass.

That's me, by the way. Oberon. Bloody silly name if you ask me, but he had just completed a particularly unsuccessful run in the abovementioned role for the local amateur drama thingy when I came tumbling adorably into his life. He goes for that sort of dramatic thing for some reason; it's a sort of triumph of enthusiasm over lack of competence as far as I can make out. Still, it keeps him out of my fur every so often.

Allow me to complete the introductions. 'Hello.' My kennel name is Parsonage Minety de Blanchard, for God's sake, and my real name is quite unpronounceable unless you happen to be a fellow Labrador. It's a noble breed, but nobility is as straw when matched in combat against the Boss's sudden whimsy in the direction of a lawn. Thousands of years of careful and conscientious selection count for zilch just because he's felt a twinge of conscience about the delicious quality of the back garden I use the term merely to identify location, it's as much a garden as I am a ballerina.

The whole thing went badly wrong when His Nibs broke the habit of a lifetime and swung into positive action. He telephoned a gardener.

Incidentally, this might be a good time to put in a plea for someone to invent a telephone that a) doesn't scare you out of your skin by going off just as you happen to be mooching past and b) allows me to hear both sides of the conversation. It's infuriating to have to work out what's going on from the series of grunts and whines from this end. After all, it might be something important and he never tells me anything.

For instance, I didn't even know he'd been phoning a gardener until this aged hornyhanded son of the soil turned up with a squeaky wheelbarrow and a selection of implements that wouldn't have looked out of place in a film about the Inquisition. Slowly he set about the complete devastation of my little Patch of Paradise. I was, naturally, outraged.

'Oi,' quoth I.

'Gerrawaywivyerr,' he riposted, taking a lunge at me with a wicked looking piece of apparatus picked at random from the wheelbarrow. I slunk thoughtfully away, not in defeat, you understand, but in quiet contemplation of my revenge.

A word of warning on looking contemplative. Don't. The merest suggestion of departure from your sunny, cheerful disposition leads to an immediate diagnosis on his part that it's time for the worming treatment, that vicious white powder that I always miss when he sneakily hides it in my favourite nibble (beefburgers, actually) and which has such an antisocial effect on my, shall we say, sanitary procedures. You'd think I'd be wise to that one by now, but it's next to impossible for me to decipher his devious intent in an expression that teeters on the gormless.

I was determined that my revenge should be of the sweetest variety, so it was some time before I completely failed to come up with my usual high standard of breathtaking, seat trembling Plan. So; no Plan. Planless. Number of available Plans? Nil.

Luckily the Labrador Guardian Angel had taken time off from his poker school and provided me with a helping hand in the Plan department in the shape of a barely visible speck of pale grey precisely in the centre of the incipient lawn. Let me explain.

Yon decrepit Adam, having toiled for what seemed like an eternity, had eventually succeeded in converting my treasure house of sensory delight into a flat, bland and squarely even plot of topsoil. Great. He was busy sowing individually counted grass seed over this regimented sod when all at once my roving eye caught sight of the Speck of Grey. As a fully paid up member of the Hunter/Retriever Class 4 Major clan, this could signify only one thing. Every instinct in my lithe frame stood up, saluted and informed me with some force that this could be no other thing than the iceberg like tip of an extraordinarily large bone.

Now there's an awful lot of rubbish bandied about on the subject of dogs and bones. The way some people go on, you'd think that Dog + Bone = Uncontrolled Excitement was a mathematically proven equation. Such a lot of nonsense. Nasty dirty things. You don't know where they've been. Catch me getting worked up about something so lacking in appeal as a large, knobbly, magnetic, delicious, unsurpassable, irresistible, unleavealoneable bone.

Oh, alright. Can I fight years of conditioning? I blame Pavlov, personally. Anyway, it was not my fault that this particular Grey Speck That Had To Be A Bone was so precisely in the middle of the square and it was not my fault that my subliminal programming took over and it was certainly not my fault that my investigation required placing the odd indentation in this otherwise virgin battalion of seed and soil. The fact that the Grey Speck turned out to be the protruding corner of an antique copy of Private Eye could hardly be said to be my fault either.

Nevertheless I was held entirely to blame. It was the hoarse cries from the wizened throat of the Ancient that first informed me something was amiss.

And I was not alone in this. By and by the Boss appeared at the back door, presumably shaken from his habitual lethargy by those selfsame cries. When there's hard work to be done, it's a safe bet that he will take to the sofa and gaze fixedly into midair; the harder the work, the more studiously he gazes. Anyway, he finally arrived and sized up the entire situation at a glance. It needed only a question or two for him to establish the fine detail.

'What the hell's going on?'

'That bloody dog of yourn's bin and gone and wrecked the 'ole bloody lot,' gasped the Ancient. 'I sh'll 'ave to do the 'ole bloody lot again. It'll take I 'ours.'

At this a sort of pale cloud passed across the Boss's visage, an event normally associated with the prospect of payment. You can always tell. Nothing can move him so briskly to despair as imminent expenditure. Honestly, you should hear him go on and on about the paltry sums he has to lash out to the vet from time to time to keep his Pride and Joy (me) in tiptop condition. I'm sure I wouldn't begrudge him the odd shilling or two had I the means.

On this particular occasion, the despair in his heart manifested itself with one of his 'Oh God, why didn't I get a cat in the first place' looks and I could read the signs of stormy weather ahead. It makes you sick, doesn't it, one slight faux pas and all that joy and happiness I'm gracious enough to provide him with goes straight out of the window.

Anyway, his eye swept the scene before him and finally lighted on Your Humble Author, quietly trying to extract some nutritional benefit from a scrap of inferior newsprint bearing some scurrilous reference to a Member of the Legislature.

'Bad boy!' he yelled, heavily emphasising the first word. 'You bad boy!' Again the same emphasis, somewhat superfluous, if you ask me. After all, I'm quite capable of understanding a concept of this simplicity in one go, you know. Mentally reaching for my How To Haul Yourself Out Of The Soft And Nasty Guide To Suitable Expressions And Whimpers, I selected the one that says 'okay, so I've been a teensy bit naughty, but I'm more than worth it, aren't I?' and tried it out on him. It's a tried and tested expression, but in this situation I felt it needed the backup of a saunter over to him and a nuzzle against the leg. I padded softly back across the embryonic lawn towards him, making sure to steer a completely different course to the one I'd used earlier in order to cause the maximum disruption. A small victory, I know, but they all count.

All to no avail. The horrors of expenditure had hardened his heart even to my best ingratiation and he completely ignored one of the finest performances in my armoury. An arm shot out, with a finger poking at a spot vaguely behind him.

'Get to your basket this instant, you bad boy.'

I found the use of the verb 'to get' in the imperative a little questionable here, but the darkness of his brow persuaded me not to make any comment on his choice of vocabulary. So I gave him my rueful, whipped expression and bounded happily off into the house towards the old basket.

I have never been able to discover why he thinks that being sent to the basket is such a great punishment; next to attacking a pile of beefburgers, it's possibly my favourite activity. But I hate to disappoint him, so I always try to look suitably chastened before plunging into the jumble of blanket, old jumper, old toys, nonspecific bits of fabric (an old carpet, I think, or it might be the remains of a slipper), scraps of The Times, examples of microscopic life forms and so on that I am pleased to call Home. I just hope he appreciates the effort I put into looking penitent while luxuriating amongst this blissful detritus.

It was this inner sanctum of mine that was to be the crux of another small altercation. That and a small female with fair hair and matching IQ and bust size. I forget the name. She arrived one evening on his arm and proceeded to fire a large dollop of disapproval in my direction with both barrels.

'Oh,' quoth she, 'you've got a dog.'

No 'hello, old chap,' no 'what a nice looking dog,' not even an enquiry as to my name, always a good conversation opener. In the time it takes light to travel across the street from the library to the home improvement shop, our mutual dislike was as broad as it was deep.

The Boss remained completely unmoved by the antagonism running rife in the atmosphere, mostly because he entirely failed to notice it. 'Oh yes,' he replied, looking proudly down at his Pride and Joy, 'had him since he was a puppy. Great little chap, isn't he?'

I must point out here that he is not normally this effusive, except when he has been enjoying a belt or two of the old Nutbrown and Frothy. His unsteady gait and daft grin tended to suggest that this was indeed the case.

'Don't like dogs,' this from the Harpy.

I think I would have bitten her out of pure distaste for her lack of grammar if I had not been overwhelmed with curiosity as to how His Nibs would handle this diplomatically demanding situation. A contest between years of Selfless Devotion and a Passing and Unwise Whimsy. I wondered how he was going to get rid of her.

"No problem, " he replied in an instant. "I'll shut him in the kitchen." I was so stunned by this cavalier treachery that I had been moved lock, stock and basket into the kitchen and the door closed before I had a chance to riposte. And let me tell you, this was a greater tragedy than you might imagine.

It had taken me months of ceaseless endeavour to get my basket moved to just the right spot in the sitting room, under the stairs without actually being beneath the stairs, if you catch my drift.

As a tempestuous puppy, my sleeping quarters had been, perhaps justifiably, very firmly established in the kitchen on

the sanitary safety that is the lino. But since racing on to Enlightenment and full Maturity, I had made the decision to move to a nicer area.

It was the Ideal Place. Good fields of fire covering most of downstairs and an interesting menu of aromas wafting from left and right, a sort of niff exchange. To be fair this was not always an unqualified delight. My nose still wrinkles at the memory of a bottle of something quite unforgivable which he got one Christmas, and which he used to splash all over his face before sallying forth to give battle down at the Horse and Bookie. Some form of insect repellent, I supposed.

All house moves are traumatic, mine doubly so. The Quest to move from Lino to Shangri La started quite hopefully with the simple ploy of tugging the Blanket from Position A (the lino) to Position B (Desirable Residence). This ploy was based on the premise that the Boss would immediately take the hint and fulfil his function in the household, viz. do the heavy work of moving the basket and all the various delights it contained. No such luck.

No sooner had I moved the Blanket and trotted back to the kitchen to supervise the removal of the basket than he calmly picked up the Blanket and replaced it in the basket, giving me one of his drooling grins that expects gratitude for a job well done. What he got was a longsuffering look of utter contempt, but he's never been very good at interpreting the subtle use of eyebrows and tail to express a point. Sometimes I wonder how he manages to communicate at all.

I tried again. He carefully replaced it again. He just could not grasp the childishly simple task that was required of him. And what made things worse was that this constant toing and froing was having a devastating effect on the special patina of the Blanket. All this airing in transit meant that is was beginning to lose that heavenly 'lived in' smell. A good blanket is like a fine claret and should be left in peace to accumulate an acceptable 'nose'. I mean to say, you don't lash out thousands of pounds on a bottle of the '53 Château Mouton Rothschild then let some silly ass keep picking it up and jogging around the nearest vineyard with it, do you? I rest my case.

After two or three days of this, I was beginning to lose my cool. I even tried nosing the basket towards the Des. Res., but if you've ever tried pushing a fully laden dog basket across lino and then across deep pile carpet with your nose, then you'll know just how unlikely the whole thing is. Honestly, I could have wept. Well, obviously I couldn't have wept but if I could have wept I could have wept.

My final desperate inspiration was to exploit his own strong lust for inertia. This meant waiting till he was otherwise occupied (soaking himself in the bath actually, it's where he 'does all his thinking', although it's a staggering revelation to me that he does any thinking at all, but no matter), then moving the Blanket together with all those treasured nicknacks that make life sweet to the Selected Spot. Surely, I reasoned, even he can't miss the implications here.

When he finally emerged, looking like something distasteful from a Restoration Comedy, he surveyed the happy pile of colourful detritus and the neatly disarranged Blanket. He looked at me. Then, at the frightening speed of a Post Office queue, realisation dawned. In a trice he had transported the basket to my new address.

I could have hugged him, but maintained my sang froid with a wag or two of the tail and the merest suggestion of a simper of delight. He goes for that sort of thing. Thus my abject horror at the prospect of relocation at the behest of this diminutive snakess in the grass (remember?).

But what to do? Salvation lay on the other side of a frosted glass door, and pretty unreliable he had proved to be, too. And what if this awful female had set her heart on making the relationship one of rather longer duration than the regulation evening at the pub (he's not really a Great Catch, you know, and gets pathetically grateful for any feminine attention, no matter what the excuse)?

This thought was so scary that I stopped chewing a doggybiccy in midcrunch. I glanced through the door. The lights were depressingly low, the music unusually melodic and he hadn't even switched the goggle box on. This was serious. I cast about for a Plan. I needed some form of selective assault, as all my normal methods of slobbering, irritating whining, eardrum shattering barking, flatulence etc, would upset him as much as her and I needed him on my side, After all, someone had to move the basket back again.

But nothing came to mind, so I started to look around for a staff and spotted handkerchief to bear away my few meagre possessions in the nomadic life I assumed would be my lot. At this juncture, however, I was distracted by a sudden flurry of activity from Behind the Frosted Glass Door.

As far as I could make out, My Lady Insignificant was informing the Boss at the top of her lungs just how much her dress had cost. This seemed odd. I'm sure he wasn't in the least bit interested and shouting rarely makes people listen to what you're saying.

Next came the slamming of the front door, so violent that it changed the channel on next door's telly, which I could just hear in the deathly stillness that followed the storm. I could also hear the Boss approaching the kitchen with a heavy measured tread. Now a measured tread, of whatever weight, from that particular worthy is so unusual that a tiny bit of angst crept into my soul.

"Well, I hope you're proud of yourself," he announced as he flung open the door. Yes, actually, but what have I done? "I just hope you realise what you've done," this with a small sigh. Come on then, come on. What have I done and how did I achieve it? Quick, I'm dying to know. Might be useful for future reference.

"She'll never speak to me again. "O Joy, O Victory! But... "Just look at this!" He held up for my inspection a small hairy item which I recognised with delight. It was a piece of liquorice toffee that I had been enjoying whilst watching a particularly boring film about Peruvian cottage industries, so boring, in fact, that eyes had closed and mouth opened. Hence the Great Escape of the toffee.

Hang on, though. Adhering to the toffee were fibres I couldn't immediately place, and I have a good working knowledge of every stitch of fabric in the house. Could it be that..? Just a second...Yes, of course. They precisely matched the togs the tiny Jezebel had been wearing. Oh bless her; she'd found my toffee for me.

Now that Exhibit A had been formally identified, I could see no reason for it to suffer the indignity of being brandished aloft, so with a speed that would surprise you in a dog of my generous yet rugged build, I leapt up and wrested it from his grasp and continued where I'd left off. Delicious.

Faced with the loss of the evidence, the Boss gurgled a bit and gasped. His eyes and mouth began to gape, He sighed deeply. It had all been too much for him. He absentmindedly patted my head and stumbled towards the stairs as if to say, 'that's quite enough for one day'.

Now I normally prefer to sleep alone in my basket, partly because of the soporific effect of my small collection of little treasures and partly because he tends to thrash about in his sleep. But that night I felt he needed the solace that I alone can bring him, so I trotted up the stairs after him. I could always have a chew of those little poppers on the duvet if I woke up in need of a nibble. There was still the matter of my basket and the Des. Res. of course, but that could wait until the morning

Chapter 2 On Exercise

Take it from me, if you want to lead a happy and healthy life, avoid exercise at all costs. No single human enterprise is more fraught with danger than this unaccountable urge of humans to leap around chasing after, or being chased by, other humans. As far as I can see, the whole endeavour is a perilous and superfluous waste of time.

Not that I object to the odd frolic in the park myself, mind you. Provided that it's not a) too cold b) too hot c) too wet d) too dry e) too windy f) too dark or g) too bright. No, under suitable conditions I quite favour an occasional dash or two in warm pursuit of a ball or stick or some such inanimate and preferably easily portable item. Inanimate, naturally, because

articles of this type will inevitably slow down and stop at some stage, allowing the pursuer to recover them at his own pace. The Boss enjoys these sorties as well. It gives him the chance to get out of the house on those occasions when, for no reason I can fathom, the Horse and Bookie is closed and he can't wedge himself against the bar. It also provides him with the opportunity to impress young females by thrusting out his pigeon chest and flexing the acorn muscles in his chopstick arms. Somehow they remain unimpressed.

Here's a tip for Brothers and Sisters who wish to bring item fetching activities to a savagely abrupt end. Run to fetch ball (or stick). Run a further 50 paces or so away from the thrower. Give ball (or stick) a jolly good slobbering. Wait patiently for thrower to come and retrieve ball (or stick), after all, if he'd wanted it so badly he shouldn't have thrown it away in the first place, should he? Observe look of distaste on face of thrower as he contemplates the handling of soggy ball (or stick). Smile quietly to yourself as thrower considers immediate abandoning of activity only reasonable course of action. Wag tail in exuberant joy.

As I was saying, I've no strong objection to a gentle burst of exercise every once in a while, as long as the amount concerned is firmly under my control. This is important. Under no circumstances should you undertake any form of activity, nor venture on any outing, unless you are absolutely certain that there is an escape clause written into the contract.

And know your enemy. For example, when the Boss rises like an awakening Kraken from his armchair, puts his pipe or his fags in his pocket, checks his short term financial position and heads for the front door, it's a safe bet that a stroll to the Horse and Bookie is on the cards. This entails a gentle amble of some 800 paces followed by a happy hour or two lying by a roaring log fire and fielding a more or less constant stream of

crisps and peanuts graciously supplied by Regulars and the better class of passing trade.

Now this form of exercise gets my vote. A lungful or two of fresh air, a chance to inspect the chestnut tree on the corner of Woodside Court and an End Result worth the effort. Common pleasures, to walk abroad and recreate yourself, as that Shakespeare chap puts it.

End Result on one particular evening was indeed the bar of the Horse and Bookie, and it was here that the first inkling of something amiss raised its ugly head, (Does an inkling have a head? And is it necessarily ugly?) The Boss was engaged in ferocious conversation with a troop of youngish coves at the bar while Yours Truly was in the very vestibule of contented kip by the fireplace. One eye remained half open in case a plate bearing Soft Touch hove into view.

This relaxed condition was suddenly interrupted by a burst of fervour in the debate at the bar. I glanced over to see that His Nibs seemed to be struggling with a particularly difficult concept, so I assumed that the conversation had turned to Money, Politics or Religion all subjects that leave him not so much in the starting gate but more back in the paddock munching grass.

Even as I watched, his expression evolved from incensed to livid, then to Decisiveness, then, naturally, to shock and finally to Grim Determination. As this is about as common as a bee orchid in Oxford Street, I switched to Full Attention Mode to find out what was going on.

"Okay, then," he screeched, at such a high pitch that I was probably the only Being in the bar who could hear him, "you're on!"

At the time I had absolutely no idea what exactly it was that they were on, nor why this state of being on whatever it was they were on should have evoked such strong and unprecedented emotions. I listened on, surveying the Scene in an attempt to pick up clues.

Let me try to draw you a picture of the Scene. Stage Right the Boss, looking more miserable than usual, sullenly sipping at his pint of Ould Spleenburster. His eyes are downcast. He has the air of a bloodhound who has been informed by a close friend that he has a personal hygiene problem. Stage Left a group of chaps, laughing and joking and slapping each other on the back like that sort of chap is wont to do. Every so often one of them takes a sip of a drink that looks just like fizzy water which is impossible, of course. No one in their right mind is going to pay good money for water, no matter how fizzy it is.

I could tell things were bad. My Noble Master is not over encumbered with a vast armoury of facial expressions and it's relatively easy to decipher the usual list - sad, angry, disconsolate, bored, distraught, suicidal etc., but beyond these his features remain more or less static. What is inscrutable for the oriental face is merely inertia as far as he is concerned.

But an expert in human physiognomy like Your Humble Author can gauge degrees of depression, and this one was a beauty. Picture, if you will, how that Roman emperor must have looked when someone nipped in to tell him that he was short by three legions since breakfast that morning and you have some idea of the gloom and despondency present in every line, blemish and wrinkle.

Got the picture? On one hand a group of happy, smiling youths enjoying life to the full. On the other hand, Middle Age dismally personified and gazing into his pint as though all the terrors of Inferno were displayed there in alphabetical order.

I needed more information than this, though. So far all I could infer was that the Boss had done or said something he regretted, but as he spends half his time regretting what he has said or done in the other half, this wasn't much of a revelation. From what I could hear, the conversation had drifted onto something called a compact disc player, which is a musical instrument apparently, and not, as you might expect, someone involved in one of those interminable sports they have on the telly. This was all very interesting, but not very helpful, so I rose and nonchalantly breezed over to the bar to prod His Lordship in the backside. I knew that this would prompt him to open his heart and tell me what was bothering him so much. It didn't.

"Oh, hello, old chap," he said. "Ready to go?"

Give that man a clear choice of two and he will pick the third. Pass him a stick labelled 'hold this end' and he will instantly grasp the other end. Stand in front of him with a placard inscribed 'this is the point' in foot high letters and he will miss it with a completeness that makes your head swim. Eheu! Would that I could pass on simple messages that he could understand instead of being forced to rely on his innate inability to grasp those subtle nuances of meaning expressed by minute twitches of eyebrow, nose, tongue, paw, ear and tail. Human language is limiting enough as a form of communication, and he is hardly an expert in that. Even a cat could do better.

So rather than suffer the ignominy of being tugged, protesting, from the bar by the lead, I decided to give way and rely instead on my powers of observation and deduction for more clues. I was also anxious that the sight of His Lordship struggling to decide whether he was coming or going, on one of those rare occasions when he can spot the difference, should not be witnessed by the public at large. I agreed to go.

As we shimmied towards the door, one of the hearties at the bar hailed us with a "See you on the squash court, then."

If you had mentioned that Attila the Hun liked to do a bit of lacework when he wasn't busy massacring people, I couldn't have been more aghast. Information regarding the innocence of Richard Nixon would have seemed perfectly reasonable by comparison. Tell me that either the Earth is flat or the Boss would play squash and I would have cancelled my round the world cruise.

Him? Play squash? Him? I mean to say, dash it all, he gets out of breath wrestling with The Times Crossword. Even at top speed he gets left blinking in the wake of old ladies with those lethal shopping trolleys. At full pelt he would have been lucky to take the Bronze Medal position in the Hare and the Tortoise race.

To say I was shocked is like saying that Hell is on the warmish side. I was dumbfounded. Stunned. If I had had vitals, I would have sent them away to be stapped. I was so completely thrown that I even forgot to make my usual liquid protest on the lamppost outside Cherrytree Lodge where that terrifying Mrs. Goodenough provides board and lodging for an entire dynasty of ravening cats. Shock turned to Fear as I slouched, distracted, back towards base. Suppose this was all real and not some awful nightmare. Suppose he really was prepared to risk cardiac arrest. Suppose...

As the road crawled lazily along under my downswept muzzle, a grim picture began to form in my mind. I was lying by his tomb, like that Greyfriar's Bobby, a Study in Designer Dejection with a howling gale whipping the falling snow into drifts against my emaciated frame. "Poor old thing," passersby were saying, "there's no one to look after him any more. His master died of exercise, you know. Playing squash, the fool."

That was it. He had to be stopped. At all costs.

This decision to act helped dispel the visions of mortality and I began to work on a Plan with gusto. Objective: Stop Boss Playing Squash. Problem: usual procedures and devices designed to make him do what he doesn't want to do or stop him doing what he does want to do no experience in stopping him doing what he doesn't want to do in first place. Ancillary factors: Pride and Honour (two particularly unnecessary qualities for humans in my opinion and much overrated, especially for out and out bimbos such as the specimen lolloping along at the other end of the lead).

These mental gymnastics lasted all the way home and right through supper, including second helpings, and it was getting on for bedtime before the beginnings of a Ruse popped into the old cerebellum. I had already considered and rejected several possibilities, such as: hiding his kit (he didn't actually have any), biting his leg (the repercussions, the repercussions), biting his opponent's leg (they'd only find someone else, and I could hardly go around biting the leg of anyone who looked like a squash player, could I? Oh, I don't know, though.)

To be successful, my Scheme would have to put the kibosh on all this ridiculous exercise lark once and for all, a one off solution simply wouldn't do. It required animal cunning, which, fortunately, I have in abundance. I'm an animal, you see.

Anyway, the Scheme I had in mind went like this: Phase 1 involved disrupting his, for want of a better term, training programme. It would be my task to ensure that he was made fully and painfully aware of the implications of all this training for a man of his physical lack of condition. This would be accomplished by waking him at first light for an early morning jog, growling menacingly whenever he attempted to eat anything that was not of a healthy, wholefood nature and snarling if he so much as glanced at his store of pipes and fags.

I would also need to practise my withering look of scorn in the mirror until it was so good even he could understand its meaning, then fire it at him every time he broke into anything faster than an amble.

That lot should take care of the physical side. Attacking the Concept side was a little trickier. If the prospect of pain and suffering was not enough to overcome his misplaced feelings of Pride and Honour, then I would resort to Phase 2 Psychological Warfare.

This entailed leaving copies of the Lancet or the BMJ lying around open at articles about death through violent exercise, although this might have proved a little too subtle for him. Another possibility would be to steer him past the Chota Peg Indian TakeAway and Grill during his evening run in the hope that the odours of exotic dishes streaming out of the ventilation system would bring him to his senses. Frankly, I find the aroma from this place a little too familiar for comfort, but he is very keen on scoffing what is somewhat vaguely referred to as 'meat' on the menu.

Actually, while on the subject of takeaways, can I enter a swift plea to whoever runs these places on behalf of us canines? It really is most frustrating to watch the Lord and Master shovelling huge quantities of nosh down his neck when it is quite clear that such fare is simply not designed to be shared with the Beloved Pet. There's nothing chuckable, you see. You don't get chips or those fabulous mushy pea fritters that a chap can entice off the plate and into the air for a spot of catching practice. The Chinese version does feature prawn crackers, I suppose, but they're pretty insubstantial.

Anyway, back to Psychological Warfare. Now, the essence of this is to unsettle the Enemy. Make him question his own beliefs, doubt what he once took for a certainty, in short, confuse and undermine him. Against a mighty and structured army, these tactics can have a devastating effect. Against six feet of leftover blancmange, as was the case here, it's a question of giving him every assistance in confusing and undermining himself. It is, after all, one skill in which he is quite definitely a Master.

As I traipsed a little further down this path of thought, I was struck by a stunningly brilliant idea. What would really unsettle the Boss would be to use his own strength to defeat him, like those judo chaps. I would heartily congratulate every feeble attempt at exertion. I would be moved to applause if he so much as rose from a chair at speed. Stark admiration would shine from my eyes if he managed even a passing imitation of a trot.

I can only assume that he had read the same book as me. There I was, anxious to flex my psychological muscles at the least opportunity, nerves taut and ready, adrenaline at full pitch, gasping for the chance to bring my Scheme into action. For three days I waited, anxious, taut, ready, pitched and gasping. For three days there was not even a glimmer of opportunity, not an iota of change in his usual routine, one that would be hard put to earn the title 'pedestrian'. For three days nothing happened.

Then on the fourth day came a telephone call, which I reproduce here verbatim to show you the sort of person I have to contend with. And although I only heard one side of the conversation, it doesn't take much imagination to follow what was going on.

"Hello?"

"Oh, hello, old man. I keep meaning to call you."

"Yes, I know. Look, there's a bit of a problem I'm afraid, and it doesn't look like I'm going to be able to make it."

"No, no. It's nothing like that. It's just that I've been to see the quack with this pain in my knee and he reckons it's something to do with a ligament or something."

"Yes, I pulled it a year or so ago playing badminton and he says it's still not a hundred percent and it'd be daft to risk it." (There are at least four direct lies so far in this conversation.)

"Yes, I know. It's a bloody shame, but there it is. Nothing I can do about it, really."

"Okay, old chap. Look, I'm sorry about this and everything, but if the doc says no go then I can't really..."

"Yup. Anyway, look, I'll see you down the pub. Bye."

The smug look that waddled briefly across his face confirmed my suspicions. He had never had the slightest intention of playing squash or anything else. All the time I had been plotting and fretting and watching and waiting, he'd been calmly stocking this lifeboat. It makes you want to spit, doesn't it? If you can spit, that is.

Then another thought hit me like an enraged water buffalo. He'd done it. He'd actually done it. He'd managed to pull the wool over my eyes.

I peered carefully at his face, all expression now erased as he optimistically perused a copy of Amateur Gardener. There was no trace of newly hatched intellect, no sign of craft or subtlety. Here was a face that Machiavelli would have trusted entirely. So how..?

Pondering the imponderable is like trying to plait porridge, so I decided to put this one down to Experience and console myself with a nibble of something or other.

Exercise? It's for the birds. Bring on the mushy pea fritters.

Chapter 3 On Nourishment

Bloody discrimination I call it. I said as much to a German Shepherd with whom I was passing the time of day whilst lashed to a rubbish bin tree outside Tesco's a week or so ago. "Bloody discrimination,' quoth I, once we had performed the standard ritual of inspecting each other's credentials, "just look at that, will you?'

The item under discussion was a huge sign on the door which stated quite categorically that, as far as this particular purveyor of comestibles was concerned, we canines were personna non grata, irrespective of colour, class or creed. 'No dogs', said the sign. Not 'No animals at all' or 'Humans only'. Oh no, our noble breed is specifically picked out and debarred by name. I suppose that if I were a cat or a warthog I would be welcomed with open arms. Or a fish.

Typical, isn't it? Yet another example of Man's Inhumanity to Dogs, like putting food into tin cans without designing openers that anyone can use, or skilfully designing cars so that they supply blasts of exhaust fumes precisely at muzzle level.

And it's not just the fact of being singled out for exclusion that really hurts, it's the lack of opportunity to guide the Boss to the correct counters, or to steer him towards the right purchase. I mean to say, he has absolutely no idea what bacon to get and his taste in cheese is abysmal.

What makes things worse is his tendency to assault the supermarket after a lunchtime spent in the Horse and Bookie stuffing a procession of Mumbai Surprise and Ould Spleenburster down his throat. This concoction has the effect of turning a mildmannered blob into something that Ghenghis Khan would cross the road to avoid. In your average supermarket he leaves in his wake the same sort of shambles that Boudicca must have done as she cut her way through the Roman legions with scythes on the wheels of her shopping trolley.

Actually, being banned from such establishments when he's in this sort of state does have its advantages: a) it saves my embarrassment at being associated with this self service maniac and b) I simply could not face arriving at the Pearly Gates and trying to explain that I had shuffled off this Mortal Coil as a direct result of an accident with a supermarket trolley. The shame of it!

To be fair, though, this frenetic provisioning does have its plus side. His Lordship's powers of selection, never particularly muscular, desert him completely and all manner of exotic foods cascade into his trolley as he belts around the Great Tesco Handicap. I think it's the colourful packaging that catches his eye. Or it might be that he always seems to shop when he's ravenously hungry, which is odd when you consider that he must have a good half a gallon of Ould Spleenburster on board, not to mention several handfuls of nuts, puffed rice, lentils, sesame seeds, raisins and nonspecific flavourings and artificial colouring agents.

And he never learns. We get home, he sits down in front of the goggle box to watch one of those old black and white films with Ronald Coleman, he falls asleep after the first ten minutes, he wakes up around teatime slapbang in the middle of an appalling hangover, he groans his way into the kitchen to investigate the possibility of some easy to make repast. By now those once alluring packages have the same appeal as major bypass surgery and by and by find their way into the Blessed Bowl. Tee hee.

It is this regular influx of foods from around the world that has enabled your Humble Author to develop a palate that is the envy of every dog I know, except perhaps that smug looking Afghan Hound that exploits the good nature of Mrs. Bartlet James at The Close.

Oh yes. One lap is all I need to establish the precise vintage of a Medoc (the '92 for me, I think). A single nibble and I can differentiate a Beluga caviar from the also rans. Sling me a black olive and my keen perception can identify it as a Kalamata or not while it's still in mid air. Pass me a beefburger and I can give you the brand, the retail outlet, the date of manufacture, the levels of fat, protein, vitamins etc., the total market size, the price and what the individual who made it was thinking about at the time. I'm somewhat fond of beefburgers, or have I already mentioned that?

Mind you, this stream of gourmandise isn't all wine and roses. The choice is rather arbitrary, and it simply isn't possible to put in specific orders for those particular items that hold the greatest appeal for Yours Truly. I might, for instance, develop an itch for a plover's egg or two only to face abject disappointment when all he can come up with is a tin of baked beans and half a pound of that terrible cheese with the brown wrapping you know the sort I mean, it's so bland and gooey it makes your teeth stick together. Top to bottom, I mean, not side to side.

And every so often he hits whatever it is that is the exact opposite of the jackpot. Take that vast tin of sauerkraut, for example or that herbal paste they use in tiny amounts to flavour spaghetti. I naturally assumed it was for spreading on toast and helped myself to a large dollop. It took me days to get the taste out of my mouth.

Now look, I'm a pretty catholic sort of chap in matters of the palate, ever keen to include a goodly range of comestibles in my diet, variety being the spice of life and all that. I'm not averse to drawing the odd bow at a venture or two.

But what really gets my goat is the total lack of ability on the part of manufacturers when it comes to labelling the produce. When was the last time you saw a label that said 'Warning - this stuff tastes like three week old coypu droppings', or 'Look out! Contents liable to get in between your teeth and drive you wild all afternoon', or even 'Don't be a bit surprised if the enclosed tuck is in no way represented by the hugely expensive and lovingly arranged studio shot we've used on the front of the packet'?

See what I mean? Completely unhelpful. Why, a really switched on manufacturer could go the whole hog and stick a label on, say, beefburgers, to the effect that the average punter may not realise that this particular delicacy is quite suitable for handing over to your favourite canine chum.

Here's how you Brothers and Sisters can rescue a beefburger from disappearing in its entirety down a human maw: First, locate the beefburger (you'll probably find it on someone's plate). Next, taking care not to rush or appear too eager, approach the Target. I find the Long Loping Forward Approach works best, as humans tend to be startled if you suddenly loom from the side, and a startled Target may clam up and draw his plate towards himself in defence. The Long Loping Forward Approach gives him time to appreciate your noble features and prepares him for the generosity he is about to display, especially if you exploit the opportunity to give him the 'deep, soulful, proud but not averse to relishing a crumb from the rich man's table' look. It's an old trick but it usually works.

A tip at this juncture. Don't crowd the Target or try to intimidate him, as this may win you one morsel simply to keep you at bay, but he will make sure he scoffs the rest of the beefie in record time so that he won't have to hand you any more. Far better to hold back so that he can show you his athletic prowess by slinging a beefie particle a good four feet or more in roughly the right direction. (Watch the look of achievement spread across his face as he successfully accomplishes this pitifully simple task but do try not to collapse with derisive laughter or you will spoil the effect.)

Right, where was I? Oh, yes. You have selected your Target and made your Approach. You should now be sitting, placid but somehow intense, with your attention directed exclusively at the eyes of the Target. It is important to capture these. Once you have these in your thrall, all you have to do is glance down at the beefie and the Target's eyes will follow yours down. When he looks up again, he will find himself still gazing into your deep, soulful, irresistible, gentle, etc., etc. peepers. That mournful yet hopeful look. That proud yet giving expression. Let's face it he doesn't stand a chance. Stand by for morsel number one.

And stand your ground. The very nature of the beefburger is working in your favour here, because not only is it almost impossible to pull off just a small bit but once the clean outlines of a beefie are disrupted by being mauled by the average human, it just doesn't look quite as appetising to them and you have a reasonable chance of a second go. It may well be that you will have to field a chip or two at this stage, but that's no bad thing provided they're not drenched in tomato sauce.

Incidentally, if you're new at this game here's a word of warning. For no obvious reason, humans are incapable of enjoying perfectly good food unless it's searingly hot, so try not to catch and gulp at the same time until you've got the hang of it. Grasp the offering lightly between the teeth, keeping the tongue out of the way. Then fan it up and down a few times to cool it. As you're unlikely to be blessed with anything sufficiently large to require much chewing, you can afford to go straight to Stage Three, viz., whopping the toothsome morsel along the back teeth and down the throat, pausing only to savour the exquisite taste on the back of the tongue. Makes you dribble just thinking about it, doesn't it?

The really Accomplished Beefburgerist, like Your Humble A, can develop the Look to such an extent that it is possible to arrest gaze, impart meaning and receive beefie at a range of some 20 paces. This requires a sort of 'Make sure you consider me every time you even mention the word beefburger from now until the End of Time' expression and is particularly effective as part of a structured campaign, especially when you have had some time to study the behavioural patterns of the Target.

One last tip before moving on. If you ever see a sort of yellowish substance parked on the side of the plate, or worse, adhering to the impending delicacy, AVOID AT ALL COSTS. This stuff hurts. Why your average, seemingly rational, human chooses to render perfectly good food inedible in this cavalier manner completely mystifies me, but be warned, it can happen.

Mind you, Humanity takes the biscuit when it comes to selecting precisely the wrong thing to do. It makes you wonder how they ever made it out of the trees.

Example: The Boss takes inordinate delight in forking out oodles of hard earned dosh on a tidal wave of hooch merely for the questionable enjoyment of a few minutes of megabefuddlement followed smartly by a day of self hatred.

Honestly, the way he moans the morning after a session and a half down at the Horse and Bookie, you'd think it was my fault that his teeth are itching and his transverse colon is trying to make an individual plea for liberty from the European Court of Justice.

Another example: Watch a Human getting ready for sleep. Now sensible creatures, even cats, face this lunge into the arms of Morpheus by taking two easy steps. 1) Lie down 2) Sleep. Sounds dead simple, doesn't it? It's obviously far too simple for our fellow Earthlings, however, who cannot even consider venturing into the Land of Nod without a good twenty minutes or more of careful preparation. First, off comes one set of clothes. A splash in the bathroom. A wander around looking like something from a 1950's horror B movie. Next, another set of clothes with stripes or dots and a pocket on the top bit. This, presumably, is supplied so that the sleeper can carry a few bits and bobs with him into his dreams. Clever stuff.

Anyway, all this is beside the point. Take it from me that humans have only the most tenuous of grips on reality and feed accordingly. Best avoid anything that arrives late on a Saturday night and in a tin foil container, this will either be an insubstantial pageant faded leaving not very much of a rack behind (and tasting awful), or it will cause you great pain, both in its ingestion and in its disposal, if you catch my drift.

And that's another thing that really gets my pip, while we're on the subject. The Boss will make sure that I always get as much food as I need 'need' you'll notice, not 'want', there's a difference (around 86%) but when the wonders of Nature and alimentation have taken their several courses, you should hear the way he carries on about the not overexacting task of taking me for my evening Symphony. (Sorry, my little joke. What I mean is a musical experience with four or more movements. Sorry. Rather tasteless really.)

To be perfectly honest, he doesn't really need to accompany me on these regular excursions, I'm perfectly capable of finding my own way around and making political comments where necessary. In fact, I think I would prefer it if he left me to get on with it but he will insist on trogging along in my wake with the air of a dead albatross to my Ancient Mariner, constantly griping about how cold/wet/hot/windy/early/late/sunny/dark it is and how he's missing the match/Archers/film/second episode/news etc. With encouragement like this it's a miracle I don't get some form of deepseated lavatorial complex

You try it. You try concentrating on the job in hand when there's a great dollop of impatient Lord and Master on the end of the lead trying to hurry you up and pretending he's nothing to do with you at the same time. Not easy, is it?

I don't know why he should get so nervous. It is, after all, my performance; he is merely in the front row of the stalls. Can you imagine it the other way round, with me pretending to be fascinated by a faded bus timetable or the particular cut of a privet hedge while he's, er, communing with Nature? No, of course not. Anyway, he always closes and bolts the door, as though someone was going to rush into the bathroom and accuse him of some terrible crime or something.

Come on, we all do it. Whether you're a mammal, fish, insect, bird or subgenus, you do it, don't you? But why is it that humans have to turn a natural bodily function into a huge production number? (Actually, now I come to think of it, cats like to make quite a fuss about it. You can really embarrass a cat if you surprise it while it's poised over its excavation.) I mean to say, look at those palatial temples to Man's nether functions that bejewel our cities and towns. If you've been lashed to the railings outside one of these places as often as I have, you'll get a pretty weird insight into Man's comings and goings, I can tell you.

For example, why is it that you only see males going into these places? I've never seen a female make use of these public facilities, so how do they cope? And why is it that blokes always look at their watches before going in? Do they time themselves?

Actually, it's a fascinating object lesson in human behaviour. Do you know, there are two quite distinct types who avail themselves of these offices? One type strides in as though he owns the place, while the other shuffles nervously towards the inviting portals as though he wants to avoid being caught in such a compromising situation. This permits the playing of a small game called Bark & Block.

Any number can play, in fact, the more the merrier. What you do is this: you station yourself outside a Public Shrine to Relief and wait for a Type Two male to approach with that unmistakeable gait reminiscent of a Thompson's gazelle wandering through the lion enclosure at Longleat at night. As the Victim is sidling up to the entrance, place your bark, I find a single, sharp bark of about two seconds duration works best. Such an attention drawing manoeuvre will completely break the Victim's nerve and he will about face and head off at the speed of light in any direction not immediately associated with the Public Comfort Station.

Although a single Bark & Block is screamingly funny, the game really comes into its own when you have a player at each similar location throughout the town. The only thing you have to watch out for is when you're on Station 7 or 8, because Victims sometimes get a bit bolder through desperation and you might have to throw in a few growls or menacing looks to keep them at bay. But a well organised game with enough committed players can keep a Victim going all day long. Or, rather, not going.

Chapter 4 On, um, Gender.

Let's face it chaps, it's all a bit of a palaver isn't it? You know what I mean, the Urge, the Force to Father, the Push to Procreate, the Insemination Itch. Alright. Sex. There, I've said it.

If there's one unifying factor throughout the Animal Kingdom, this is it. The only Odd Man Out, as it were, is the two legged member of the terrestrial tribe, who stands alone in his remarkable lack of success in this particular pursuit.

It works like this: the Human Male receives the Mating Call and immediately sets about selecting a suitable breeding partner. He visits the watering hole where females of the species are likely to congregate in sufficient numbers, makes his selection and starts his Display. This can take many forms. He may festoon his body with gold knickknacks in the hope that these blatant shows of wealth will appeal to the greed instinct in the female, providing, of course, she isn't put off by the complete lack of taste. He may thrust out his chest and strut about the place to demonstrate his virility and imply that he would make good breeding stock. Unlikely, I would have thought.

Then there's the Intellect Display, where the male affects spectacles and a copy of The Times in the hope that this will make him look interesting. From the few examples of this type that I've seen, most would improve their chances by taking off the specs and holding the paper the right way up.

Perhaps the most amusing type is the Warrior, who sincerely believes that getting completely anaesthetised on gallons of hooch and indulging in fisticuffs with whoever comes to hand is the best path to a female's heart. A somewhat doubtful premise if you ask me. In most cases it's the best path to a stomach you could rest a tea tray on and a face mildly reminiscent of overcooked cabbage.

Having identified the Players, let us now consider the Action. Actually if you want a good giggle, keep an eye out for this Procedure in pubs and similar houses of liquid entertainment all around the land, mostly on a Saturday night.

Male as described selects female and approaches same. Makes Display. Gets rebuffed. Retreats to secure position (the bar usually, or in a cluster of his fellow Hunters). Sulks awhile. States loudly that selected female is a right horror when you get up close/sexually questionable/doesn't know what she's missing/frigid/toffee nosed. Replenishes alcohol level. Approaches Contingency Female. Gets rebuffed, naturally, because no one likes to be Contingent. Retreats to defended position again. Sulks. Restates opinion of female in question and females in general. Inserts excess alcohol. Picks fight with innocent bystander in order to reestablish Manhood. Gets chucked out and heads for Indian Takeaway with his chums.

What a carry on, eh? But even if the male has some tentative success in making contact, this is just the beginning of a trauma of such profundity it makes you wonder how Mankind ever made it to the second generation. I mean, it's all very well establishing first contact, but it's still a long and rocky path from base camp to the summit of mating activities.

The means that the male has at his disposal are too many and various to be catalogued here, but most seem to depend on some form of nourishment, from a cheap box of chocolates to a full blown multicourse dinner complete with aperitif, a choice of wine with each course and a liqueur to follow the Stilton. Odd, when you come to think of it. If I'd enjoyed a nosh the size of that, the last thing I'd want to do is bounce up and down on top of, or underneath, my dinner guest.

Chocolates. Be damn careful with these, or you could find yourself in deep trouble. I remember being seduced by a dainty example of this genre, beautifully packaged and lovingly moulded and shaped, only to discover that the centre had the consistency of Cornish granite. A great deal of perseverance yielded nought but the most foul tasting something or other imaginable to go with the throbbing ache I had in the jaw line.

Now, I expect you're wondering what comes next in this tragic tale of the male's Quest for Conquest. Well, so am I. As far as I can make out, the male has to pay for his brief moment of glory by signing over all his past, present and future possessions to the lady in question. I suppose that, in most cases, this is no great reward for whatever it is that she has to go through, but it makes you think.

Like any other venture, of course, this wholesale handing over of life and limb to one's Beloved does have its risks. I mean to say, what happens if the Chosen One turns out like that unspeakable Mrs Jamieson at the newsagents? Awful woman. You can well understand why Mr J. elected to shuffle off this mortal coil rather than face that termagant for any length of time.

Whoever is responsible for the Cosmic Plan should jolly well make sure that that sort of thing doesn't happen. And while they're about it, some assistance for the Boss would be greatly appreciated. Poor chap, he has as much chance of procreating as I have of coming up on my Premium Bond. (Yes, I have just the one. Pathetic, isn't it?)

He has all the sex appeal of preformed concrete. His line of chat sounds like it was written by Dostoevsky when he was feeling particularly depressed. You need logarithm tables to calculate his success rate. Compared to him, Quasimodo was a real puller. To be blunt, calling him a dead loss borders on flattery.

Listen, if he'd had a pound for every Conquest he'd made he would have just about enough to put down a deposit on a parking fine. For a bicycle.

And what throws his complete and comprehensive failure into even sharper relief is my own magnificent record. Pass me a bitch in season, a loose hand on the lead, a handful of the right pheromones and my hit rate is 100%

I do my best for him. I introduce him to hundreds of ladies in the street with the old lead entangled round the legs ploy, or the 'gimme a stroke or I'll cry' look. It never works.

I like to get him involved. Why, only the other day we were resting in the Horse and Bookie, me by the fire, him by the bar, when in glid a delicate bloom accompanied by what appeared to be a pet orang utan. The latter wore a T shirt announcing that he was a Miami Dolphin, which was odd, because whatever stitch in the evolutionary tapestry he occupied, I could tell at a glance that he was no dolphin. Anyway, the Sweet Young Thing looked like she could procreate, so I mooched over.

"Oh, look, Wayne! Isn't he a beauty?" she said, showing such keen perception I knew I was onto a winner. I accepted with grace the proffered handful of peanuts, noting with satisfaction her generosity of spirit. Some people, faced with the same situation, make a token offering of one or two of the smallest nuts they can find right from the bottom of the packet where the salt collects, but this worldly saint came across with a handsome fistful. And they were dry roasted too. I quite like them.

As I munched contentedly, I began to muse over the best tactics for the given scenario. She looked so comfy where she sat that I decided to get the Boss involved with my 'come hither and make it snappy' call which starts as a sort of rumbling basso profundo and ranges swiftly through a brace or two of octaves to somewhere around a G above middle C then ends with a staccato forte ma non troppo. It is unignorable, and before the windows stopped rattling, the Lord and Master was by my side. Stage 1 complete.

"Is he yours?" breathed the Sweet Young Thing. "Mumble." This conversational jewel from the Boss. "He's a beauty isn't he? Isn't he a beauty, Wayne?" "Grunt." said the orang utan or whatever.

"What's his name?"

"Um, Oberon."

"Oberon? That's a funny name." I could have kissed her.

"Oh? "

"Grunt. "

"Here, boy! Here, Oberon!" Another helping of nuts. Spurred into action, I started to whack the Boss in the back of the knees with my tail in order to manoeuvre him into a good position. Normally a good position for the Boss is recumbent, but there's an exception to every rule. As usual, he missed the point with startling efficiency and began to back away to the safety of the bar. I knew I would lose his interest, such as it is, if he got his snout back into the Ould Spleenburster and his elbows wedged into a soggy drip mat, so I reverted to Desperate Measure Number 7 and rolled onto my back.

"Oh, look, Wayne! He wants his tummy tickled. Do you want your tummy tickled then, boy?"

With this, she plunged a cool, bijou mitt onto the old undercarriage and began stroking. Oh, boy.

At this juncture I would like to point out that upside down is not an easily tenable position for a dog of my stature and dignity, because a) it's not very comfortable, b) it leaves you very vulnerable to attack and c) you bang your head on the floor if you look up suddenly to see what's going on. Rarely will you see Your Humble Author in this situation. But for the sake of this professional Tummy Tickler, I would have swum the Hellespont on my back, let alone just lain there and taken it. She had the sort of lightness of touch which would go down well at a Convention of Microsurgeons, with an eye for hitting exactly the right spot.

The obvious delight oozing from the old visage was having its effect on the other protagonists in this small scene. The orang utan's face started to pucker with disdain, and what neck he had to start with disappeared completely, so that it looked as though his head grew straight out of his shoulders. His breathing became laboured and he started to edge forward on his chair.

The Boss had been reversing into the bar all this while, his face a mixture of guilt, lust, fear, confusion and Ould Spleenburster. His backward progress was brought to a painful halt as he caught his Achilles tendon on the rail that runs the length of the bar.

I pressed on with my enjoyment of the abdominal attention, all the while considering ways to begin weaving together the Destinies of the Boss and the S.Y.T. As far as I was concerned, she would do very nicely for us; one has to be so careful, doesn't one?

Eventually, I decided the time had come to set some form of plan into operation. Reluctantly I righted myself and ambled over to His Nibs, all the while casting glances over my shoulder to the Delicate Bloom as if to say 'It's ok, he's with me and he's quite nice when you get to know him.' A bit of nifty glancework had the two of them looking at each other, and before you could recite the complete works of Dickens, the Boss had grasped the situation and made his move.

"Um, would you like a drink?"

I'm afraid that I've never been particularly good at Latin; we all have our blind spots, I suppose. But I remember vaguely that there are words used in questions depending on whether you are expecting the answer 'yes' or the answer 'no'. This question fell neatly into the latter category.

"Lovely. Brandy and Babycham, please."

"Ouch." (He didn't actually say 'ouch', but I could hear him thinking it.)

At this, I became aware of a dark, rumbling noise from the direction of the orang utan. As it grew louder, it was possible to identify it as a fragment of human speech, struggling to get out. I waited patiently for the birth.

"Oi!"

Stand aside, Shakespeare. Move over, Marlowe. Take a hike, Hemingway. You've all met your match. But soft. There was even more to follow.

"Oi, you!"

My dear, such dialogue. Can it be Coward reborn? Such economy of style, such pungent repartee. I tingled in anticipation of the next gem to drip from this Master. How could I have been so crass as to confuse this wordsmith with an example of the lower simian orders? More! More!

"Wassyoregame, pal?" A talent for foreign languages as well! What a genius!

Mind you, my dear old Boss was ready with his own biting wit. You can't get much past him, you know.

"Um?" he said, slapping the ball powerfully back into the enemy's court.

The anthropoid rose slowly to his feet. He had to do it slowly, I guessed, simply because his brain could not make the necessary equilibrium calculations quickly enough for him to rise any other way without overbalancing. Or it might have been because he would have subjected himself to extreme trauma in trying to cope with a sudden change in his angle of viewpoint.

Something in the air informed the non participating members of the assembly that there was something afoot. Have you noticed the way that humans go out of their way to witness vicarious violence purely for the pleasure of complaining about all the vicarious violence they are forced to witness?

Anyway, somebody turned down the volume control on the hubbub of conversation in the bar, and several pairs of eyes swept the room to identify the source of the atmosphere before settling on the Boss, the Sweet Young Thing, the Neanderthal Presumptive and the Star of the Show (Me).

As a natural performer, I found this undivided attention perfectly satisfactory, but the Boss is one who takes to publicity like a breeze block takes to gliding. He doesn't even like catching sight of himself in a mirror, which explains a lot. Still, Down Centre is my natural location in a set piece of this kind, so I shimmied over to the feet of the anthropoid and sat down. As I had expected, this confused him, in the same way that lying down in front of a charging rhino is supposed to stop them in their tracks because they can't make out what's going on and so nip off for a bit of vegetation instead. I have not actually heard of anyone putting this theory to the test, mind you.

"And get dis mutt outer me way." I transcribe phonetically, and it took even me a few seconds to work out what he had actually said. Evolutionary throwbacks like him should come complete with a simultaneous translator.

The very moment this precious row of pearls had fallen from his lips, bearing in mind the slight delay required for interpretation, I knew I had won. The Boss could breathe easy, because a White Knightess was on her way.

"Oh don't be so stupid, Wayne. Sit down, do. You're embarrassing me."

If anyone doubts the power of the female, the sight of this sweet and elfin creature soothing the savage beast with just a few choice words and the correct use of the eyes and eye furniture should convince them. I felt like applauding at this point, but that's a surprisingly tricky manoeuvre when you need all four limbs for optimum stability. Instead I gave her a huge grin and a mammoth tailwag. I think she got the message.

But you don't have to be pretty and petite to hold total sway over your chosen partner. The bludgeon works as well as the rapier for keeping human males under control. And if you still remain unconvinced, I suggest you spend a weekend with Mrs Jamieson at the newsagents.

Chapter 5 On Offspring

It is a well known fact that we Labradors are 'good with children', putting up with all sorts of abuse and maltreatment, smiling through when we are being tugged by the ears, ridden on, prevented from making forward progress by a small hand on the tail. Our patience is saint like, our tolerance is legendary. Wrong.

The next time that little terror from the house on the corner opposite The China Syndrome Chinese restaurant belts me over the head with my own rubber bone, I shall explode a perfectly good myth. I shall also confound NASA by launching a small child into orbit without recourse to expensive rocketry.

Am I alone in the Universe in my disdain of children, that undersized, overindulged, undercontrolled, undisciplined rabble whose sole aim in life is to create disruption at every turn?

'But you were a pup yourself once,' I hear you say. True. But that was hardly my fault, and I made damned sure I reached Maturity and Enlightenment at top speed. Oh, I'll admit the occasional misdemeanour in my extreme youth, the odd 'accident' on a Persian rug or two, maybe the merest nibbling of a priceless bit of antique furniture, hardly noticeable at a distance, perhaps a slight interment of a half set of silver plated cutlery, but these were merely examples of flaws in my training. Nothing to do with me.

Okay, that time I pulled the tablecloth off without having the opportunity to see that the table was fully laden could, I suppose, be perceived as a tiny bit naughty, but there was no malice there, merely exuberance.

No, if you want Mischief Personified, look no further than the nearest sprog of either gender, especially the ones that look like those cherubs favoured by particularly maudlin producers of greeting cards. If there's one thing that bitter personal experience has taught Your Humble Author, it is that the cuter they look the harder they poke you in the nose.

And what's more, if you turn round and poke them in the nose there's all hell to pay. To this day, I sting from the injustice of an encounter with one of the Boss' nephews, who was, presumably, a particular fan of the more lurid of the Western movie genre.

With his Colts tucked into his belt, he moseyed over to the corral to climb aboard his favourite steed, in this case Your Reluctant Author. A light leap and he was astride, ready to ride

the range. Instant lowering of the old hindquarters, however, saw the Lonesome Cowboy sprawling i' the mud, bawling his eyes out and rightly so too, if you ask me.

But his sobs eventually touched some chord deep in the canine heart, because I foolishly wandered over to lend assistance. My reward was a wallop on the hooter from an angry, and extremely grimy, fist. It hurt. But what hurt even more was the cascade of abuse and remonstration I subsequently enjoyed from the outraged mother, who assumed from the evidence that I had contrived to push her tiny hooligan into the mire on purpose. O Gelert, thou shouldst be living at this hour!

And as if that wasn't bad enough, there was an 'atmosphere' in the house for days afterwards I think the Boss got a severe case of the earbend on my behalf; we are, after all, a nation of dog lovers.

The thing is, you see, you can never win with kids. Do what they want you to do and you get into trouble. Don't do what they want you to do or do what they don't want you to do and you get into trouble. The only difference is in the source of the trouble into which you get.

Take that time when I was persuaded, against my better judgement I might say, to venture into the strictly private Parkes Wood by a small army of Visigoths from the local comprehensive. The original objective, as I understood it, was a good, old fashioned game of 'off the ground he', where whoever is 'it' can transfer their 'ittedness' by touching someone with at least one foot on the ground. My role was to run the boundary and arbitrate on marginal decisions.

If you've ever seen the effect of one of those hurricanes in the bayou country of the Southern United States, you'll have some idea of the havoc that can be wreaked by a tribe of small people working to a common end, viz. the complete destruction of anything within a radius of about five hundred paces. I remember once observing the church hall after a Kiddies tea party, which had the air of San Francisco after the earthquake. Personally, I think it was San Andreas' fault.

You know how it is. What started as Off The Ground He very quickly degenerated into a preadolescent version of Isandhlwana. Savage impis of sprog swept menacingly through the woods before rising as one to fall upon the defenders of a clump of striplings near the brook. It was magnificent. It was war.

It was brought to a very sudden halt by the arrival of a gentleman in tweeds with a very silly hat and a very unsilly double barrelled shotgun under his arm. He looked unamused.

"What the hell do you kids think you're playing at?" bellowed the Person.

Interesting, isn't it? Even under what could be described as stress, people still manage to exercise their native literary forms like this bloke coming out with a Rhetorical Question, just like that. Next thing you know, the woman from the Post Office will be whipping out an occasional Oxymoron or a swift Synecdoche when the queue starts to get restless.

There was only one of him; there were lots of us. Had we but taken to our heels, he would never have caught any of us. Yet, somehow, the baleful, metallic gleam of the four eyes fixed on our assembly (two human, two 12 bore) contrived to drive any thought of flight from our communal mind. It was Authority, and therefore to be harkened unto.

"Well?' prompted Authority.

"We weren't doing nuffing, Mister." This from our self appointed Spokeschild, after one of those pauses that that Pinter bloke is so keen on, a pause so pregnant that you half expect to see the midwife hovering in the background with her sleeves rolled up.

"We was just following after that dog," piped another perfidious treble, indicating Your Humble Author with not more than an inch of finger poking out from a grubby duffel coat sleeve.

"That's right. We seen him belt into the woods and went in to get him out again," fibbed a third Quislingette. "Cause it's private here, you know," he confided darkly.

Have you ever been so incensed that you found it impossible to do ought but sit and stare, with your jaw

dropping and your brow furrowing like a millpond subject to a
sudden breeze? I sat and stared, with jaw dropping and brow
furrowing like the aforementioned millpond faced with the
sudden breeze in question. I felt violated, betrayed, too stunned
even to whimper my innocence. Every child's hand was turned
against me. I was a scapedog.

Look, I really don't want to dwell overlong on the upshot
of this little enterprise, far too painful. Suffice it to say that
they no longer execute animals in this country, and that I got
off with a severe talking to and was 'gated' for three days when
the news of my gross misdemeanour finally filtered back to the
Boss. Frankly, I don't suppose he really cared one way or the
other, but he likes to pretend he's in control every now and
then. It lulls him into a false sense of superiority.

But the whole episode taught me a salutary lesson about
sprogs viz. don't trust them an inch. They know no nobility of
spirit, no sense of decency, no feel for justice or chivalrous self
sacrifice. They inhabit a dog eat dog world of their own, if
you'll pardon the expression.

I'm going to have a little moan here, with your indulgence.
You've all gone to a lot of time and trouble to develop this

language of yours, paltry though it is for communicating any but the simplest of concepts. Perhaps someone could explain to me why you need to sprinkle it with similes and metaphors degrading us canines, like 'dog eat dog', 'leading a dog's life', 'she's a real dog/bitch' etc.

It really is most unfair, especially stacked up against such as 'lithe as a cat', 'cat's whiskers', 'cat that had the cream' etc. Come on, team, how about a bit of linguistic authenticity, like 'as idle, vicious, vindictive and irritating as a cat', or 'straight as an Airedale', 'bright as a Bulldog', 'as pleased as Pug', 'the wisdom of Sealyham'?

But to return to our sheep, I simply must tell you about the Day I Was A Hero In Amongst The Snow. Now I don't mind snow too much, providing it's not more than ankle or so deep. In fact, it's quite fun to larrup about in, skipping sideways to leave confusing tracks, getting a good load on the end of your tail and flicking it at innocent bystanders, traipsing straight into the sitting room and watching the little white paw prints melt into little puddles of water, writing strange cabbalistic signs around lampposts and trees.

Great fun, actually, especially when you can plunge straight into a nice warm basket as soon as the novelty wears off. But there is a major drawback. A layer of snow has a severely deleterious effect on the powers of the old sniffer and it makes it inordinately tricky to establish the exact location of those delicate little knickknacks one buries i' the ground from time to time. Of course, you can always employ sophisticated triangulation techniques to provide a rough idea, but pinpoint accuracy is impossible given the movement of the earth's magnetic field.

It's a right bugger, isn't it? Bear in mind the fact that the old proboscis was not up to its normal level of efficiency and add to this a sudden and all consuming desire for a nibble of a particularly exciting bone section only recently interred, and you will understand why I was rooting around the school long jump pit in the first place.

You know how it is when you get a craving for a special something. Absolutely nothing else will do once the whim is riveted firmly in the bonce. Your mind is set on a cherry flavoured blancmange, and even free tickets for the RSC at Stratford cannot distract you from your purpose. With an obsession like this occupying centre stage in the consciousness, the worst thing that can possibly happen is for some inanimate agency to stand between you and your Objective. And what makes it even worse is when the hurdle in question is well within your ability to leap given normal circumstances. So. Snow, reduced olfactory prowess, brain scrunching desire. Got it?

Naturally, I ran through a trial triangulation, hampered by the fact that a) there was no sun visible and b) I had chosen a particularly flat and featureless landscape in which to lodge my little treasure. The best I could do was to identify a possible area covering some three hundred square paces, and even Schliemann would have thought twice about excavating that lot.

I needed a point of reference, some landmark which could narrow the area of search. Ideally, something which could jog the memory, you know 'Ah yes, I remember considering the possibility of christening that sapling when I'd finished burying the bone, and what's more it was over my left shoulder and one hundred paces away.'

But there was no sapling. I was faced instead with a uniform white expanse, with only my own somewhat haphazard tracks violating the virgin purity of the snow. I sat down for a think. This was a mistake.

My only consolation for a cold, wet bottom and an unfulfilled need was the thought that, if I couldn't find the bloody thing there was no chance of some interloper getting there first. We dogs, although a loyal and noble genus, are not averse to nicking each other's bits and bobs should the opportunity arise.

I decided to venture a trial dig, a sondage, if only to elicit clues from the soil type and structure; you get a feel for this sort of thing when you're a dog. I was, momentarily, astonished to discover that I had hit sand, rather than the loamy, friable soil I was expecting. Having discarded the possibility that I had either landed on Omaha Beach or had somehow wandered into the Gibson Desert, I quickly realised that this was, in fact, the long jump pit of which I spake earlier. Not a great help, it must be said, but it did give me a kind of reference point. It was at this moment that a movement caught my eye.

It's funny, isn't it, the way that a tiny movement can grab the attention while a slightly more expansive movement, such as a neutron bomb going off or Krakatoa exploding, can go by completely unnoticed? Such was the case here, with my keen senses picking up a slight resettling of the snow over to my right. It had to be something after my bone. With a couple of bounds, Your Humble Author arrived to investigate, ready to kill, or at least maim, to protect my little treasure from this ravisher, whatever it was.

Now, you have to be a bit careful when plunging the soft bits of your muzzle, unsighted, into a snow drift. Not only is there a chance of frostbite, but there is also the possibility that something, or someone, may be standing by underneath with sharp attachments. Speaking as one who has had a rather nasty confrontation with a largish crab in a rock pool near Mevagissey, I can testify to the axiom about looking before you leap, or in this case, lunge.

It was awful. Half of me screamed to assault this ravenous bone section purloiner at all costs while the other half said, 'hold on, check your background readings and reconnoitre before choosing your best method of attack'.

I waited over the spot in a state of rare indecision. Whatever it was seemed quite large and quite long, with no clue as to which end was the biting end. It moved again, very slightly, in a non aggressive sort of way. I thought I'd give it a nudge in the middle, logically the safest bit.

There was no response to this pre emptive challenge, so I began to paw away some snow to give myself a wider field of fire. After a few digs, a piece of dark blue material was revealed. It was a human.

I couldn't understand why a human should be trying to do me out of my bone, but I was prepared to put forward a strong

argument about legal possession and the Theft Act. For this, I required the attention of the entire person rather than a segment of outer apparel. I continued to dig.

What finally emerged was a child, male, of some five or six summers. It was dressed in the blue coat and finely encrusted with frozen snow. It was not paying attention, which was a problem because I needed to know if and how it had found my bone and what its intentions were. It needed to be awakened for cross examination.

When I eventually got it to wake up, it broke out into an earsplitting howl which quite made my eyes water with its pitch and intensity. This was not playing the game. How was I supposed to question this infant if all it could do by way of reply was bawl its head off? Not fair, not fair.

And it simply wouldn't stop. I tried stuffing a paw over the mouth, prodding it in the chest, licking its face to attract attention all with no success. It was starting to get on my nerves, and I was getting very close to calling the whole thing off and diverting myself with a good chase of the tabby from the farm when a small knot of people hove into view. They approached with speed, finally forming a small cluster around the infant. One of them picked it up and started to make strange cooing noises you would normally associate with any species of waterfowl on a Monday morning.

Another set about patting my head and stroking my muzzle with rather too much enthusiasm for my liking. Still, it's always nice to be attended to, so I accepted the adulation while waiting for an explanation. After a while you get used to complete strangers making free with parts of your body, but it's unusual for a whole gang of them to cross a snowcovered waste for the undoubted privilege of doing same.

After the initial fuss had died down, it was possible to make out one or two facts which went some way to explaining the situation. Apparently the child in question was not trying to rob me of my bone after all, but had gone missing in much the same way; presumably it had also been buried until required, which struck me as being a sound idea spoiled only by their complete inability to locate the spot afterwards simply because of a light dusting of snow. Hopeless.

Anyway, it appeared that they were jolly pleased to retrieve the infant, and their delight manifested itself in the shape of one of those chewy jobs designed to look like an old shoe. Very satirical, I'm sure, but quite tasty. I bore it before me like a standard as I was ushered back home by the grateful crowd, to be met on the doorstep by the Boss. I must confess that I quite enjoyed the role of the Hero Returning, an event only slightly marred by the fact that His Lordship was not even aware that I'd left. But once he had been appraised of the wonderful Thing that I had done, he handed over his Final Accolade.

'Well done, old chap,' he said, and scratched me on the noddle, just on that bit that I can never reach for myself. Bless him, the perfect end to a perfect adventure.

Never did find that bone, though.

Chapter 6 On Seasonal Variations

If there's one thing guaranteed to create Strife and Dissension in this household, it's the Season of Goodwill. It usually starts around October, when he gets all grumpy because the local supermarket begins moving things around to make room for the impending avalanche of nuts, dates, boxes of crackers, tins of biscuits, chocolates, tangerines and plum puddings. For someone who has trouble finding their way around the bathroom without a route map, all this relocation causes monstrous confusion and frustration.

Throughout the Autumn he has a mental crisis. He can never decide how involved to get in the Christmas spirit you know the sort of thing; does he go completely overboard and get a tree with decorations and such, or does he keep it low key and festoon the place with the dozen or so Christmas cards he gets?

I'm afraid I'm really no help to him with this Eternal Question, simply because I can't make head nor tail of any of it. It's an activity exclusive to humans, in spite of anything you may have heard about robins, reindeer or the assorted beasts of burden that feature in the manger scenes.

And as an event devised by humans, it's bound to include most of the following features: 1) somebody will make money from it 2) it will be in all the papers 3) you'll get sick to death of it on the telly 4) no two people will agree about what it all means.

I suppose I approve of all this present giving lark, although in my case it's mostly present accepting. It's just a pity that the Boss has absolutely no idea what to hand over to Yours Truly by way of Yuletide Offering, and I always get something nibbly but uninspired. I blame the Marketing departments of dog nosh manufacturers. They put together selections of tired lines that don't move very well for the rest of the year, stick a picture of snow, or a bit of holly on them and brand them as doggie Christmas pressies. This nifty bit of packaging then takes the place of thought and imagination for such as the dear old Boss, so it's all Wimpole Street to a Chinese orange that

Christmas morning will provide a host of second class quality munchables.

Still, there's always Christmas lunch to look forward to, if you don't mind being prodded in your sensitive parts by some youthful relative, or scared out of your wits by an inconsiderate cracker puller, or silenced for the duration by an ill timed invasion of a box of toffees. And you can't even enjoy a good after lunch howl because they're all struggling to stay awake long enough to watch the Queen's Speech and shush you if you so much as yawn.

I think it was last Christmas, or maybe the one before, when I first found out that I was an Excuse Not To Go To Someone Else's House For Christmas Lunch. I just happened to be within earshot every time the phone went and chanced to hear him turning down three aunts, a cousin, the bloke from down the road and that hideous woman from the drama thingy who, he tells everyone, keeps chasing him. (Actually, I'd love to meet her, if only to make friends with the guide dog she's bound to have.)

"Sorry, can't really make it," he'd say to them all, "but I've got to look after Oberon."

Rot. Leave me a twenty four pound turkey, access to a source of fresh water and an open back door and I can look after myself. It's just that he can't stand spending any length of time away from his own little corner of the Universe unless he really has to. Except for the odd meander to the Horse and Bookie, of course.

And he very rarely goes away anywhere, and never without me in tow. Do you know, I have yet to have the pleasure of spending a few nights in kennels. I feel that this is a serious gap in my education, and what's more, it sounds like I've been missing out on a lot of fun. A good cross section of chums lying around available for a good chinwag, young ladies on call to gratify one's slightest whims, a menu stuffed with Lucullan variety, a bracing daily amble with the chance to sample a host of new niffs and staging posts. Of course, you get the odd homesick hound that howls for his blanket, but the impression I get is that they all have a jolly good time and I think I'd like to give it a whirl.

Not much chance of that, though. It's not just that the Boss was at the back of the queue when they handed out senses of adventure, it's also the same old problem of trying to crowbar a pound or two out of his wallet. I'm sure he could go without a pint or two of the Ould Spleenburster so that I could spend a few days of pampered relaxation at the local Dogotel (who thinks of these names?).

Sometimes his total lack of enthusiasm is a bit of a worry, like that time he turned down the chance to tour with his drama clique in a production of The Tempest. When I say 'tour', it was actually only one performance to be staged in a drill hall in Bournemouth, but it's quite exciting when you're used to declaiming The Bard from a stage made of old pallets at one end of the Infants School gym.

Once again, I got the blame for that one. He couldn't possibly go away for the night and leave me on my own, I would be sure to pine/make a mess/have a sudden and unprompted heart attack/knock his half finished jigsaw off the dining room table/molest his Sunday Best slippers etc.

Frankly, I'd be more concerned about him being on his own for the night, especially when you consider his usual performance on New Year's Eve. It's the only time in the year when he's guaranteed to visit the Horse and Bookie unaccompanied, and a jolly good thing too, if you ask me. I have the dubious pleasure of witnessing the Result, I'm thankful I don't have to sit through the Process as well. Watching him ladle X pints of Ould Spleenburster between his tonsils, where $X =$ any number greater than 10, then proceed to link arms with the thing on the bar they use to take the corks out of wine bottles to sing 'Auld Lang Syne' in the mistaken belief that he has joined a circle of revellers is a sight that could haunt me till the archangels blow the Final Whistle. The mental image is bad enough.

Mind you, I don't get off scot free. He invariably hauls a selection of old cronies back with him in the wee small hours to 'have a couple and finish off the year in style.' This is a use of the word 'style' that may be unfamiliar to you. In this context, it generally means each informing every other one that they're the finest person on God's Earth, that the country's going to the dogs (no, it doesn't mean we're taking over, it's just another example of the English language's inhumanity to canines), that things used to be so much better when they were lads and that most of their wives don't understand them. My sympathy is with the wives; I can't understand them either.

Pretty soon this impromptu World Reorganisation Committee Meeting degrades into a 'who can stay upright the longest' competition, starring his bottle of Irish whiskey and whatever music cassettes are at the top of the pile. There was one delicious year when I was treated to the prospect of a group of semiconscious Horse and Bookie Regulars sitting around in deep and solemn conversation for an hour and a half to the strains of 'Teach Yourself Modern Greek'

I like to keep a low profile on these occasions, it's far too easy to become either a target for physical abuse or to get buttonholed by someone who wants to explain their personality problems to me at great length and at point blank range. Frankly, I don't know how these agony aunts can stand it, but then I suppose they don't have to suffer the outpourings of a tormented soul directly into their ear and at full volume. One bloke went so far as to lift my ear flap so that I could really enjoy every misery of his life's story, together with a fine spray of whiskey, tobacco fumes and half chewed peanuts.

It's not until the following morning that I get my own back. As it's the First Dawn of the New Year, I feel it my duty to wake the Boss at the earliest possible moment and appraise him of the Promise of the Future by leaping onto his bed, at around stomach level. This catapults him into a form of wakefulness, and is followed by a severe face licking to complete the task. When I am quite sure that he is fully conscious and able to appreciate every ounce of his hangover, I sneak quietly back to the old basket to continue my own slumbers. After all, I've been kept awake half the night, haven't I?

I must say, though, whoever organises Christmas and New Year and all that does a good job. As soon as it's all over, they have the January Sales so that you can fight your way round and buy all the things you were hoping to get for Christmas. The massive crowds in the shops put you off returning the unwanted stuff until it's too late to bother; the supermarket shelves now contain nothing at all except Christmas trimmings at half price that nobody wants or can even face.

The programming on the telly is so awful for the first three weeks or so of January that it gives you a chance to catch up on all the films you recorded over Christmas. There was one film called 'The Great Escape' which was absolutely marvellous I think they should show it every Christmas.

At the very moment the bright snow of Christmas has turned to the brown slush of winter ennui, our spirits are revived by the appearance of colourfully packaged Easter Eggs in more or less every retail establishment in the High Street. Actually, I'm not too keen on Easter, ever since an episode in my extreme youth when Someone Who Should Have Known Better left a whole chocolate egg lying around unattended just begging to be assaulted; all I had to do was clamber onto a kitchen chair, scramble up onto the table and unearth it from under a pile of bank statements and credit card slips. It may have been the exciting rustle of all that paperwork going onto the floor that prompted my particular devilment that day, or it may simply have been the seductive aroma of the chocolate, but whatever it was, I scoffed the lot, including a fair percentage of the wrapping paper.

It must be said that this was not one of my best ideas. I spent two days feeling extremely ill, two days feeling extremely stupid, two days feeling extremely sorry for myself and two days feeling nothing at all. When feelings reemerged, they took the form of a growing determination never to overindulge in anything ever again. It's the closest I've ever been to a New Year's Resolution, even if it was shortly after Easter.

Easter's only claim to fame, as far as I'm concerned, is that it confuses the Boss even more than Christmas does. He never knows whether or not he should be sending cards, and if he should, to whom. He is aware of Easter eggs, but can't decide what the age threshold should be for receipt/non receipt of same for his infant relatives. The next problem he has to face is whether you give anything at all to the aforementioned nephews and nieces once they are perceived to have passed the age when they receive Easter eggs. Complicated, innit? There should be some form of Guide to all this nonsense, so that everyone knows where they stand and you don't get frosty glances from your aunt because you didn't send her a card/Easter egg/bunch of flowers/bath salts etc.

The only good thing about Easter is the fact that it presages the Spring, when all of Nature yawns, stretches and warily opens an eye to see how the year is getting on. With all the shenanigans at Christmas and Easter, I'm surprised she doesn't turn straight over again and go back to sleep. I quite like Spring. Not only is there a freshness in the air and new life and all that stuff, but the soil is easier to dig and you can go out for a wander in the afternoon without striding purposefully into small bushes in the dark. It's still a bit parky, though, and it invariably chucks it down as soon as you're more than a thousand paces from any form of shelter.

Getting caught out in the rain is almost a hobby as far as the Boss is concerned, and I have to suffer as a consequence. There's some Controlling Force up there which says, 'quick there he is, let it rip,' and before you can say 'forgot your umbrella again, didn't you, you brainless prat' the whole

landscape takes on a damp feel and a darkened hue and somebody turns on the cold tap.

At an instant, welcoming earth turns into clinging, cloying mud and it really does get everywhere, you know. What isn't splashed on you by passing pedestrians soon works its way up your legs as you plosh along on your sodden way. Sodden rain.

Hey ho for the Summer! Season of buzzing insects, fluffy clouds, twittering birdsong, screaming kids, herds of tourists and caravans and roof racks jamming the highways and byways as far as the eye can see.

I got chatting to a Cavalier King Charles Spaniel one Summer while his chaps were in Boots trying to find something for the kids' terminal car sickness.

He was suffering the ignominy of a caravan holiday and loathing every minute. No sooner had he gone to the trouble of marking out one bit of territory around this Hell on Wheels when they upped and moved the whole caboodle off somewhere else, forcing him to rescout, repace, redefine and remark. An awful waste of time and energy, it seemed to me, plus the fact that there must be thousands of acres of Claimed

Territory up and down the country with no one in residence. Such a waste of perfectly good marker fluid. If the Boss even so much as considered thinking about the possibility of speculating on the chances of turning over in his mind a fleeting whinny concerning the purchase of a caravan, I'd bite his leg. Fast.

Still, Summer isn't all bad. There's that satisfying click of willow on leather which means that the Horse and Bookie Regulars have chased the vagrant sheep off the Green and are going at it hammer and tongs with those spry youngsters from the Axe and Cleavage. Ah, cricket, the Sport of Gentlemen, not to mention the assorted geriatrics, vagabonds and hooligans who turn out for the dear old Alma Mater. It makes the Sunday afternoon game look like a remake of the Longest Day, only more dangerous. Fortunately, our side is blessed with a built in safety valve. Me.

As soon as I see anything I consider to be 'not playing the game', I nip over and swipe the ball. This leads to a rather one sided chase where a dozen or so wheezing Casualties of Life's Injustices come hacking after Your Humble Author with rather more hope than performance. When I have judged them to be sufficiently knackered from this exercise, I graciously allow them to retrieve said sphere, safe in the knowledge that they are now far too shattered to get up to any malarkey.

Hence the game can continue at the languid and gentle pace for which it was designed, and everybody can concentrate on working up a thirst for the visit to the pub and the ritual

'good game, but I thought we were rather unlucky with the wicket. It didn't really suit our style of attack.'

I think it was the dear old Swan of Avon who mentioned something about Summer's lease hathing all too short a date. Whoever it was, they hit the nail slap bang on the bonce; the whole thing is over and done with before you get the chance to notice it's arrived. The minute your back is turned, the leaves are falling and the supermarket shelves start to fill with Christmas stuff again.

There's not much more you can say about Autumn, except that it's a good time of year not to stop for a kip under a tree. I did it once, and woke up with a very soggy undercarriage and bits of foliage spoiling my otherwise sleek outline.

Still, maybe I'll get that rather smart quilted jacket in the window of the pet shop as a Christmas present. And maybe Darlington will win the UEFA cup.

Chapter 7 On Training

I demand a medal. It began when I decided to conduct an experimental training course in an attempt to bring the Boss even more to heel; I got the idea from a bloke called Pavlov, who was successfully trained to respond to certain stimuli by a bunch of dogs that happened to be around the place at the time. Anyway, my idea was to get the old Lord and Master to come up with the necessary nibbles on a 'need now' basis, rather than having to wait until he could fit it into whatever passes for a planned daily routine in his fevered noddle. The thing is, you see, that the canine stomach clock is a very intricate mechanism, and leaves no room for error or delay. Once it goes off, immediate feeding is of paramount importance and any other minor distractions, such as an earthquake or an invasion by aliens from another star system, simply have to take second place.

This is perfectly obvious to sensible chaps like you and me, of course, but it has yet to bore its way through the bulkhead that shields the mind of You Know Who. Most of the time he gets it more or less right, it must be said, merely because he can recognise a threatening gesture when he sees one, and a few growls plus a bared tooth or twain usually manage to divert him from whatever he was about to do when he should have been giving his full attention to my bodily requirements. But it's all so much effort, when all I should have to do is issue a mental edict that it's that time again and same form of scoff should be forthcoming within seconds. And with seconds, preferably.

Now as I see it, in order to build up you first have to knock down. So to get the ball rolling, I embarked on a system of manoeuvres designed to create so much confusion and self doubt in the murky waters of His Lordship's consciousness that he would simply give up and start again, permitting me to ink in a few minor amends.

You know the sort of thing I mean; you steadfastly gaze at the end of a pointing finger instead of at whatever is being pointed at; it always drives them wild, that one. Then there's the one where you circle round and round before lying down somewhere, which is really only effective if you always go round clockwise until they get used to it and think how quaint it is, then suddenly reverse direction and start making widdershin spins.

Then there's the old mirror ploy. That's the one where you stand next to someone who is admiring themselves in front of a full length mirror. Nine times out of ten, their reaction will be to invite you to look at yourself, partly to ease their own guilt at appearing so vain and partly because it makes them feel that they're bringing you up to their own level of sophistication. So to bring them straight back down to your level, merely affect not to notice your own reflection, no matter what they do to try to make you. This one will disconcert even the most well adjusted person in seconds flat. With someone as badly out of tune as the Boss, it's a pushover.

Of course, we all have our favourite ways of throwing our human co residents out of kilter. I favour the 'odd behaviour' method, like deftly catching objects thrown at you for a while, then suddenly sitting there quite placidly and innocently gazing at the thrower as the object sails over your head unnoticed. That one really gets them going.

I used to know a Welsh Border Collie who lived with a family that had an attractive teenage daughter. The family called him Jock, and to get his own back he adopted the following device: whenever a young beau called to pay court to the daughter, Jock would bound over in feigned joy to greet them. Then he would examine their feet and groin, in that order, bringing his nose up sharply to the latter. Border Collies have quite a sharp bone in the muzzle, with the result that the girl's parents thought that all their daughter's suitors were called 'ARRGGHHOOJH', and that she was strangely attracted to males who seemed to gasp a lot and spend their time bent double.

Then there was a Pointer whose favourite pastime was to grasp between his forepaws any upright leg that came within range and, well, jiggle. This was a marvellous idea, because not only did it thoroughly embarrass the owner of the leg, it also thoroughly embarrassed his Beloved Master, who was invariably up the other end of the lead looking the other way with all his might.

There's one ruse suitable for the more petite dog, and that's the one where you're out walking, feel like you've had enough for one day and wish to be conveyed back to your basket with all speed and in comfort. What you do is to use your skill and judgement to select exactly the correct pace to cause the maximum annoyance to your companion, i.e. too slow for them to crack along at the speed they want, but too fast for them to inspect hedgerows, scenery, shop windows etc. I have a very good friend who is a West Highland Terrier and an expert in this particular field, capable of judging it to a T. As soon as he feels he has had sufficient exercise he goes into the routine described above and within ten to fifteen paces his walking companion is so cheesed off that he is picked up, nestled in the arms and borne home.

I tried it once. Didn't work. I think the Boss would rather stay annoyed than try to struggle anywhere with my lissom form in his arms. There are limits, you know.

Retraining can be a long and arduous task. It took me nearly two weeks to get the Boss into a fully receptive state i.e. barking mad, if you'll pardon the expression, by using the devices outlined above as well as one or two others, such as being prepared to kill for a piece of brie one day and avoiding it like the plague the next.

The Boss started to go round with a permanently haggard expression. Every time he tried to tie his shoe laces, they snapped. Every time he wanted to warm some milk, it boiled over. He ironed in some of the sharpest creases you've ever seen in precisely the wrong places on his shirts. He spilt red wine on his favourite light grey trousers. I had him.

It works like this, you see. He was having such a bad time that every event that didn't go cataclysmically wrong became a shining oasis in a desert of misfortune. All I had to do was ensure that good things happened immediately after he had handed over the nosh, so that he would begin to associate the act of feeding me with things going right for a change. Eventually, he would respond to the awfulness of life by slinging the odd munchie my way, and as life is fairly awful most of the time, this meant a guaranteed and regular supply. So far, so good.

Making things go right for him was easier said than done, of course. He does seem to go out of his way to make life as hard as possible for himself, never taking the easy way when a completely illogical and laborious way will do instead. He should get fan mail from Disaster Funds.

My first task entailed calming him down a bit, but only after meals (mine, that is). This was the easy bit; all I had to do was eat what I was given, keeping most of it within the actual eating area and all of it within the kitchen; normally I like to spread it about a bit, it makes it go further. Then, for about an hour, I would behave quite normally, making sure to give him no trouble at all. After that, of course, it was back to the Reign of Confusion. This was most effective, and had him looking forward to nosh time almost as much as I did. A promising First Step.

What I needed to do now was to put into his mind the suggestion that life would be sweeter if he fed me more often. I could cope with that, and it would make him feel that he was controlling his own Destiny. It's important that the subjects of sophisticated psychological experiments have the illusion of being in charge. If they think for a moment that they are being manipulated, they get all huffy and won't play.

This phase was partially successful. The only problem was that his anxiety to feed overcame his powers of selectivity, and I found myself faced with all manner of fare, a large proportion of which I wouldn't have given to a cat.

Still, he was erring on the right side, just needed a bit of fine tuning. So I let it ride for a couple of days which was

about as long as I could stand this constant barrage of Rich Tea biscuits, cold baked beans, pineapple chunks, prawn salad, Chinese wholewheat noodles and cottage cheese (with chives) that the Boss was ladling in my direction before taking the next Step: Moderation Training.

It's quite simple. If he gives you what you don't want instead of what you do want then you do what you want whether he wants you to do it or not, and it's only when you get what you want that you do what he wants providing it's something that you want and even then you might not do what he wants just to keep him on his toes. It's all a matter of Awareness, really.

Some people can get very sneaky at this stage, and pretend not to want something they do want so that you'll do it out of spite and fall into their little trap. This sort of negative logic requires forethought and cunning, however, so it's never been a problem I've had to face. At least, I don't think so.

Moderation Training needs to be very finely judged, or the Subject could simply revert to his original behaviour and mess up all the hard work of disorienting him in the first place. In my case, it meant gently easing off the 24 hour supply of comestibles without making the Boss go completely deranged at the sight of his Little Bundle of Fun actually refusing food.

A formidable task, as I'm sure you'll agree, and I nearly made a very bad mistake. You see, I'd got to the point when I simply could not face another helping of dry muesli and peanut butter and the old gastric control centre was saying 'it's never worth it, old chap. Ditch this lot quietly where the Boss will never find it.' This I proceeded to do, keeping an eye, an ear and a nostril out for the Dear Chap.

I had chosen for my hiding place a pair of suede shoes that he'd received one birthday from one of his aunts. They really were quite frightful, and even with his questionable taste in attire a still, small voice had warned him that they were simply not on. They had slowly worked their way down from the wardrobe in his bedroom to a small storage area conveniently near the bin in the kitchen until he could work up the courage and energy to place them in said receptacle.

All I had to do was nose this horrendous concoction, which had agglomerated during its undisturbed rest in the Blessed Bowl, across the line and heave it into a shoe. Then I had to break some off and heave it into the other shoe to avoid giving the game away with the amount that was poking out through the lace holes.

Fine. No problem. By and by he would pick up the shoes and drop them in the bin, thus saving me from the torture of having to eat the stuff or the shock of him discovering that I did not necessarily wolf down every scrap graciously provided by My Lord Bountiful.

I had reckoned without the cruel sense of humour of Whoever it is that runs things round here. No sooner had I tucked away the last morsel of evidence than the phone rang, and the Boss hove into view.

From the horror in his voice and the panic on his face, I deduced that this was not necessarily the best of news. I did not fully realise just how bad the news was until he came to whimper into the instrument that he would be pleased to see her for tea and no, of course it wasn't too short notice and yes, he still had the dog and yes, he'd make certain it (it!) was kept well away from her. I added two and two. It had to be That Aunt!

She's never liked me. Frankly, I don't think she likes him very much, so why she had decided to pay this sudden and unprecedented visit was quite beyond me. But one thing was for sure, he'd not see old age if she turned up and caught him not wearing the shoes she'd so thoughtlessly burdened him with.

Unwittingly, I started to pant. It would not take the Boss all that long to work this out for himself and soon he'd come looking for the foregoing footwear, prior to plunging a tentative toe into a mixture which by now had the constituency of builder's aggregate. Oh dear.

I didn't have the time or the wherewithal to gouge the offending material out of its new home, nor could I safely remove the shoes and dump them over a cliff somewhere. Apart from an unreasonable dearth of cliffs in this part of the world, I had no means of exit from the house, and would be hard put casually to conceal a pair of shoes anywhere inside while he was rushing round like a demented Dervish in a fevered attempt to tidy the place up for the impending visit.

The shoes themselves started to exude the magnetism of a road accident; I couldn't keep my eyes off them, which was a pity, because my abject terror was compounded by the sight of a dark stain that was beginning to spread from the toe end. Presumably the peanut butter was beginning to degrade and all those natural oils were making a bid for freedom through the leather. Oh dear, oh dear.

Now a lesser mortal might have given way to panic in this situation, but we Minety de Blanchards are bred to keep a cool head in a crisis. I decided that the best way to hide anything in this house was to place it directly into the hands of the Boss, and did exactly that one shoe at a time. The dignity of the moment, I felt, was somewhat spoilt by the fact that I handed him one while he was frantically trying to remove caked soap and shaving cream from the basin in the bathroom, and the other while he was wandering about like a ferret in a trance trying to work out what to do with the first one.

He looked at the shoes. He looked at me. He looked at the shoes again, this time taking the trouble to peer inside at the solidifying mass of organic produce. He looked at me. Slowly, a mischievous smile spread across his face like slurry across a farm yard. I didn't like that Smile. I'd obviously missed something important.

"Who's a clever chap, then?" he said, leaning over me with the shoes tucked behind his back. He set off towards the kitchen with me at his heels. I was completely lost, I admit it, and was fascinated to see what he would do next.

As we reached the kitchen, the front doorbell rang. The Boss hurriedly stuffed the shoes into the bin and headed for the door, wiping vestigial muesli from his fingers. A tall figure loomed through the glass darkly it was, indeed, That Aunt.

"Hello, Aunt," said the Boss, on opening the door and confirming my suspicions. "Do come in, won't you."

Why is it, I wonder, that aunts are invariably so formidable? After all, the only qualification for the job is to have a sibling that bears offspring, so how is it that your average aunt comes over like Tamburlaine the Great on an off day?

This one was no exception. She handed My Lord Unnerved a withering glare, reloaded, and handed it to me before sweeping through the door like a Chieftain Tank at full throttle. It was not until she had settled into the Boss's favourite armchair that she made her initial pronouncement.

"Come here."

We came.

"Sit down."

We sat.

"Pay attention."

Attention was paid.

"I'll come straight to the point. I think it's high time you took a wife."

Stap me vitals, stone the crows, smack me in the kisser with a piece of steamed halibut and I'll go to the foot of our stairs. Well, wouldn't you be surprised? How would you feel if some relation of yours dropped in one day and calmly invited you to go immediately to Devil's Island for the rest of your days without passing Go or collecting the regulation double century? I can tell you, all of a sudden the shoes took a back seat.

"Wwwwhat?" whimpered the Boss.

"High time," continued That Aunt. "As a matter of fact, I have a girl in mind for you. I forget the name, but her father's in the City."

"Wwwwhat?"

"Oh, do stop whimpering. Anybody would think that no one has ever been married before. So smarten yourself up, get rid of that damned thing and start making this place suitable for decent people to live in."

You will be scandalised to hear that the 'thing' in question was none other than Your Humble Author, busy cowering behind the sofa. There are few things that can generate such fear in the loins as a certain kind of human female with her mind made up. Nevertheless, I decided to take a peek to see what was going on.

That Aunt was happily choosing new décor as she looked about her. The Boss had the sort of expression that makes Kafka look like an end of the pier song and dance man. He caught my eye, and his face just said 'help'

Tricky. I mean, I felt like going straight for her throat, but I hardly think that would have saved the day. But what could I possibly do to haul him out of this knotty little problem? It was a Desperate Situation. It needed Desperate Measures. As luck would have it, these are my favourite kind. I slunk out to the kitchen, retrieved one of the shoes from the bin, trotted back into the Situation and plonked it directly onto the lap of That Aunt. While she was busy being aghast, I nipped out and got the other one. I have an orderly mind.

Her displeasure manifested itself in several ways. First, she went red, then purple. Next, she rose from the chair like a Minuteman chugging out of a missile silo. The shoes, neatly garnished with some old cabbage leaves and a potpourri of fag ends and wet tea leaves, fell at her feet and stuck to the carpet. Her gun turret swivelled round until the Boss was in the sights.

"If I live to be one hundred I never, ever want to see or hear from you again. Is that quite clear?"

"Squeak, Aunt."

"How could I have been so mistaken about you? It's quite obvious to me now that there isn't a scrap of decency or moral fibre in you."

"Squeak, Aunt."

"I am leaving now. I shall put this episode, and you, entirely from my mind. Do not try to contact me. Oh, you're a very sad disappointment. If only your poor mother were here..."

"Squeak, squeak, Aunt."

The final manifestation of the displeasure of That Aunt came a little while later, after she had left the house taking most of the lintel with her as she slammed the front door. A sheepish looking Boss reemerged, with that Smile back on his face. He tickled me under an ear.

"Well done, old chap." he said, "I may never hear the end of it, but without knowing it, you've saved me from a Fiancée worse than Death."

Happy to oblige, I thought to myself, especially as I had also saved myself from a bit of a tight spot vis a vis a pair of shoes and the contents thereof.

So, a medal if you please. Anything distinctive will do.

Chapter 8 On Species

The discovery that you are not the only species on the planet is a trauma from which you never really recover. As you become more and more aware that the place is neck deep in all manner of things that walk, crawl, scamper, swim, fly, slither, glide, hobble, lurch etc., you begin to wonder what Unseen Agency came up with the idea in the first place. More to the point, you begin to question the wisdom of anyone who can go to all the trouble of designing and colouring in a wasp and then provides it with a defence mechanism that makes it one of the most socially outcast creatures around. Not including estate agents, of course.

I well remember, as a young puppy, the struggle I had to come to terms with the fact that I was a member of a species which was not only not unique, but not even in charge. I've learnt better since then, mind you.

It's a well known fact that behind every Great Man there's a Great Dog. Everyone in a position of power and influence needs that Very Special Chum to give them solace, companionship and the odd word of advice on how to run the country, fight the war, win the election, get the Budget through

HENRY VIII   ROVER

the House and so on. It's just rather unfortunate that this Great Dog happens to behind a somewhat Lesser Man.

With all the support and comfort available from a canine pal, you may be surprised to learn that some people choose to link their fortunes with members of other species. Like cats. An abomination on the Face of the Earth, if you ask me. They toil not, neither do they spin, in fact, they don't do a great deal of anything apart from lying around preening themselves or kipping in precisely the most inconvenient place that they can find. That's when they're not nicking your food or sitting smugly just out of reach on a fence or whatever.

You wonder why we chase cats? I'll tell you. Vengeance. Getting our own back for years and years of doing all that comforting, supporting etc. while the moggies just sit around getting all the attention for just sitting around.

Mind you, there are some cats you would be wise not to chase, especially if you're on the smallish side. Take, for example, that Tom who used to reside somewhere down Bowerbridge Lane until his people upped and moved. He was a Holy Terror with permanently extended claws and a face pitted with battle scars. He had dark eyes in a completely black face and you couldn't even see him at night unless he was smiling. He rarely smiled.

I only tangled with him the one time. I was taking a gentle stroll along a hedge at the bottom of the 'garden' when I caught sight of something small and furry heading across my field of vision at high speed. Immediately behind it, and gaining fast, was something decidedly large and furry.

As I watched this drama unfold, my heart went out to the poor little mite at the front of the rapidly moving queue, and I decided to intercede on its behalf. With a bark and a bound, I joined the queue at the back, safe in the knowledge that the cat would recognise his Master and scurry away to annoy someone else. He didn't.

He stopped dead, turned right round and hissed. Obviously the damned thing didn't know the Rules Dogs chase Cats; Cats do not turn round and threaten Dogs but I was prepared to be tolerant and overlook this glaring breach of etiquette. Unfortunately I don't speak Cat, so I was unable to point all this out to my antagonist in a calm and rational exchange of views. I gave him a mildly menacing bark instead to show him who was boss.

He hissed again, arching his back and flattening his ears against his skull. Actually, this is quite a frightening sight, especially if you're on the receiving end. But we Labradors have Courage bred into every thew and sinew, so I took a pace forward. So did the cat.

The whole thing was getting beyond a joke, and as I had fulfilled my Main Objective, namely the rescue of the tiny scampering thing, I decided to call it a day by frightening this precocious moggie out of his skin. To this end I gave him a full throated, window rattling, buttock clenching series of barks, growls and teeth. The cat remained firmly tucked inside his skin and completely unmoved in every respect. There was nothing else for it. My Ultimate Weapon. The Snarl.

Nothing can stand up to a really good Snarl. I've known

grown men join a supermarket checkout queue on a Friday evening before a Bank Holiday rather than face a good Snarl. Whole empires have tumbled before the mighty wrath encapsulated in a Snarl from a top class practitioner, and you're hearing this from one who holds a Black Belt in Snarling. So I snarled. The cat continued to hold his ground, although I'm pretty sure I saw a whisker twitch.

So. He wants a fight, does he? Fine. Okay by me. No problem. Right, then. Go on, then. I'm ready. Come on, then. What are you waiting for? I advanced, slowly. No reaction. I advanced a little more, narrowing my eyes and mentally loosening the six gun in my holster. Still no reaction, obviously this greenhorn didn't know the Correct Form for the Shootout.

This might have gone on all day if we hadn't both been distracted by a magpie, which skimmed the ground between us. It completely threw my concentration and I think it had a similar effect on my opponent, because when I looked back at him, the arched back was starting to droop, the fur on the back of his neck had settled down to the merely frenetic and the ears were starting to perk up again. The bloody thing had lost interest.

Actually, so had I, not that I was particularly keen to

engage in fisticuffs in the first place, being something of a pacifist by nature. Still, one problem remained. One of us was likely to lose face by being the first to leave the Lists, and the old Pride of the Minety de Blanchards simply would not allow that Someone to be me. I hoped that the cat didn't share the same family pride, or we could have sat there gazing at each other all night.

And to make things worse, now that the excitement had died down, I could hear my stomach softly calling me with the message that it was getting very close to Refill Time. Honestly, the pressures of life, it's a wonder I don't get neurotic.

The cat, meanwhile, had reached a similar decision vis à vis Troughtime, and did not share my sensibilities about Pride and Honour etc. He turned round, let me have an excellent view of his bottom and trotted off with his tail making a question mark in the air as a comment on the whole business. Can't say I blamed him.

Apart from the very rare moggie like this one who will spoil the Fun of the Chase by not running away, there is another type of cat it would be wise to see off while you remain calmly stationary, and that is the one I call the Misleader. You know the sort of thing you get up a good speed, come within a tenth of a thou of catching it, and it suddenly jinks through the tiniest of cracks under a hedge or something. Or it hangs a swift left and leaves you belting off in a straight line chasing fresh air for all you're worth. Some of them will even lead you over trick surfaces, the kind that will allow the passage of a Bantamweight cat, but will immediately engulf the paws of us canine Heavyweights. Like wet concrete, for example, or freshly tilled soil.

And then there's the sort of cat that just sits there and tries to outcute you, like that smoky grey Persian thing that invariably adorns the lap of Lady Gwendolyn Gledhill from the Lodge. Admittedly she's a somewhat elderly lady and tends to sit about a lot, but I've never seen her without the blasted ball of fluff stuck there gazing stupidly out from under a whispy sort of topknot; presumably the thing is surgically implanted. If you could spare the time to wait around until the Honourable Lady decides to shift from one chair to another, you'd probably find that either it has no legs at all or that it hangs down in transit like a kind of sporran.

Not forgetting, of course, probably the Greatest Threat to Man or Beast the kitten. Kittens are a sort of four legged, furry SAS unit. For creatures of such a tender age, they have an uncanny knowledge of the world of Antiques and Fine Arts, selecting only the very best porcelain to knock off the mantelpiece or the most delicately wrought curtains to clamber up. They will shun all artificial scratching media, preferring to sharpen their incipient claws on the choicest upholstery.

But this taste for overt finery completely deserts them during that unfortunate phase in their development between weaning and litter training, No more outward show, no extrovert demonstration of achievement, no honest display of their newfound ability to lighten their load, as it were. No, these tiny hoodlums opt for Camouflage, Secrecy and Deception, with the result that their surprisingly sturdy messages can lie undiscovered for days, assaulting more or less all the senses except sight.

As far as I can tell, these dangerous bundles of fluff have found the exception to the Physical Law that states that Matter can neither be created nor destroyed. You stuff an ounce of kittynosh in one end, wait a few minutes then gasp in disbelief as a good pound and a half completely misses the litter tray from the other end. Nasty, and dashed inconsiderate if you ask me. Even in my most untrained youth I had the decency to address the National Press in the way that seemed most suitable, with none of this hole in the corner stuff, if you see what I mean.

But the worst thing about kittens is that they can do no wrong as far as humans are concerned. A platoon of these minimarauders can devastate the average three bedroom semi in around five minutes flat, but instead of earning the perpetrators a good belting as you would expect, this wanton vandalism generally receives nothing harsher than a 'they're so sweet, you can't stay cross with them for long, can you?'
At least when kittens finally deteriorate into cats you can chase them; Honour will not permit the Chasing of a Kitten. Besides, you can never find the little beggars when you want them.

I suppose it's possible you lot have already spotted the fact that the World is not exclusively stocked by dogs, people and cats. There are birds, for instance, smallish bods that float around in the sky or prance around out of reach squawking their heads off when you're trying to get some kip. Some of them go so far as to take up residence in people's houses, although why they should prefer this to a life of Adventure and Excitement, with the constant threat of attack, dismemberment, exhaustion, electrocution, poisoning, icy cold weather and starvation completely escapes me. No sense of fun, I suppose.

It's an odd way to make a living, being a residential bird. They give you this little house of your own to live in, but use see through bars instead of proper walls so that you don't get a minute to yourself. You get food and water, of course, and a mirror to play with. Great. Of all the possible items with which to share a domicile, I imagine a mirror is quite possibly the least useful.

Apart from the fact that the average beast looks a sight first thing in the morning, it's a bit tricky to perform an effective toilet when you've only got a collection of wings and spindly legs. The really, really lucky birds get a little bell that goes tinkle.

Mind you, if you think being a bird is strange, you should try being a fish. There you are, casually gliding along underwater and trying to get up some speed for a double piked somersault with full retraction and a half flip, when you run slap bang into a bit of water that's so hard it hurts your nose. Now you and I know this is the glass around the tank, but when you're a fish inside said tank, there's no way of knowing in advance where the water ends and the living room begins. There ought to be some form of warning, like a sign that says "Beware! Aqueous environment ends in 20 flurgles."

A 'flurgle', by the way, is a unit of linear measurement roughly equivalent to three and a half light flicks of the tail when there's no assisting current. Or did you already know that?

When you're going at it hammer and tongs it's surprising how quickly you can cover 20 flurgles, especially if you're not really thinking what you're doing. Fish rarely think what they're doing. This may go some way to explaining how they can be fooled into considering that a sharp metal hook with a bit of feather tied to it is an irresistible delicacy.

If you want a really daft animal, I reckon the horse takes a lot of beating. I mean to say, if you sat yourself on my back, stuffed a large metal bar in the old mush and directed my progress by yanking on the bar and kicking me in the stomach with your bootheels, you'd get pretty short shrift I can tell you. I don't know how they can put up with it.

Actually one sort of horse has the misfortune to have the Worst Job in the World; teaser stallions, I think they call them. Anyway this poor low class thing works in a stud farm and his role in life is to chat up the mare, take her to the theatre and out to dinner, listen to her problems, suffer the abuse of involuntary courtship and all that sort of thing until he has won her over, then at the very moment he is on the brink of enjoying his Rich Reward, as it were, they hoick him out the way and sling in the aristocratic stallion to finish the job.

This is just one more example of the rough treatment Man doles out to the beasts of the field, forest, air, sea, kitchen etc. Like those beagles they use to test out new brands of fags. They make them smoke around forty a day from Monday to Friday then nip off home for the weekend leaving the poor blighters without a fag between them. They must be gasping by Sunday night.

Let's face it, Mankind uses us animals for his own purposes. He shaves sheep to make himself clothing, without a thought as to whether the sheep might get a bit nippy and like its coat back again, quite apart from the indignity of it all. He gives cows all the trauma of having offspring but denies them the moment of pleasure, and as if this wasn't enough, plugs them into machines so that they can't even enjoy the cool roughness of the milkmaid's's hands on their nether bits. Good taste prevents me from mentioning what Man does to snipe before they're popped into the oven; all I will say is that if anyone tried that trick on me I'd have their hands off.

It seems that everywhere you look, Man is having a good time being beastly to animals. It's a good job we dogs are around to redress the balance a bit.

Chapter 9 On The Media

I'm afraid I have had little use for newspapers since that Glorious Day when I became Officially Housetrained (except for The Times, of course, I like to spend ten minutes or so solving the crossword clues and trying to work out what those funny little black and white squares are for).

It was a wonderful day. The Boss was proud of me, I was proud of me, everyone clustered round us in the street, attracted by the rare sight of a beaming smile on the normally featureless physiognomy of the Revered Lord and Master. I felt a bit like a débutante at a Coming Out party; it was my first experience of being the Centre of more Attention than the odd cooing visitor to the house.

But even in my formative months I had a strong feeling that, in some cases, my efforts were enhancing the contents of the newspaper rather than spoiling them. Not that it's particularly easy to read a paper when you're sitting on it, but some left more of an impression on me than others, if you see what I mean.

I must say, the Boss was very proper about the whole exercise, always checking to make sure that there were no pictures of the Royal Family in the firing line, and encouraging me to make political comments on his behalf if the right personality was featured. In time I became quite an expert in current affairs and was able to pass my own comments, although I had to be somewhat swiftish if my views disagreed radically with his.

The other bone of contention between us during this phase of my development happened on Tuesdays. This was the day that he finished with the colour supplements from Sunday, having successfully bypassed the mail order ads and failed to learn anything from those interminable reports on the lifestyles of the famous. This meant it was my turn and it was an experience I grew to loathe. You just can't get a good grip, you see.

The bloody things keep sliding about the place, loose inserts fall out, the staples are invariably badly fixed and poke up in the most awkward places and some of the colour work is shockingly out of register. Makes your eyes go funny if you look at it at close quarters, and when you're a young pup thirsting for knowledge, close quarters is the only choice you get.

I think it was my distaste for these slimy interlopers that prompted me to pull out all the stops and complete my housetraining ahead of schedule. I still tremble at the memory though, and when the mood takes me, I'll savage the occasional copy out of pure spite. On a Tuesday. It helps to brighten up the front end of the week.

Newspapers are okay for puppies, but for me the ideal medium is the good old wireless. When I'm in a relaxed mood, replete and content, there's nothing to beat a jolly good lie down on the rug with an ear aimed at one of those marvellous plays, or a fascinating insight into metal crystallography or what have you. I quite favour those panel games as well; you know the sort of thing I mean, you get four fulltime panel gameists and a humorous question master and let them loose on any subject that takes your fancy, such as music, sport, theatre or whatever. Add an audience that gets in for free and so feels honour bound to enjoy itself and will laugh fit to bust at the slightest excuse and you have a winning formula.

Then there's the Archers, of course, one of the few soap operas of any description that actually features canine stars, although I did find that Captain of Blessed Memory a rather unconvincing character. I don't know any Bull Terrier of whatever breed that would have put up with the sort of nonsense ladled out by that chap at Grey Gables. And I would certainly have had Peggy Woolley's fingers off by now. Still, the dear chap did show one spark of initiative with one of Mrs Antrobus' Afghans.

I quite like the occasional quiz as well, like Brain of Britain, although it is so frustrating when the entire panel doesn't know the answer to the simplest of questions about Heraldry or Astrophysics etc.. You get so carried away you find yourself bellowing the answer at the wireless, not that that does much good.

I suppose I'm quite fortunate in having a Boss who enjoys listening to a proper wireless station. I remember howling in sympathy with a Rottweiler whose people submitted him to a diet of mindless chat liberally speckled with the most appalling 'popular' music. I don't know who exactly this horrendous row is popular with, but my chum the Rottweiler is definitely not on the list.

Don't get me wrong, I quite like some nonclassical music; a bit of Blues, perhaps, or psychedelic West Coast rock, a dash of Irish jigs and reels, a portion of the beefier types of Folk music, I have fairly catholic musical tastes. This is fortunate, because every so often the Boss gets the moist eye of Nostalgia and slings on some jiggy nonsense at full blast, and it's terribly bad manners to howl the place down when he's trying to relive the past.

You have to be tolerant. He is, after all, more or less a Child of the Sixties. (You could put forward a strong argument to the effect that he's also a Child as far as every decade is concerned, but let it pass.)

Mind you, I will not stay in the same room as Grand Opera. I'm sorry, but it is a performance medium that simply passes me by on the other side, probably because I can never make out what they're all going on about at such length. I can't really see the point to all that unintelligible singing when the whole thing could be done so much simpler with a few lines of dialogue in a language you can understand.

I have the same problem with ballet. I mean, I like the music, that really nice chuggy bit from Prokoviev's Romeo and Juliet always gets me going, but I can't cope with all that leaping about on tiptoe and over people's heads. It all looks remarkably dangerous to me, a bit like a carefully choreographed traffic accident without cars. I've never seen it live, of course, dogs not being particularly welcome in Places of That Sort of Entertainment, but from what I've seen on the telly I think I would prefer it if they put ballet on the wireless instead.

Talking of the telly, I wonder if I might address myself to Someone in Authority with the following plea: either a) can we have just the one channel or b) can we ban the use of remote control devices? The reason for this plea is simple: every time I start to get the hang of some complicated spy thriller or psychological drama, he admits defeat and switches channel to a programme closer to his intellectual level. Like Benny Hill. This wouldn't be so bad if it wasn't for the fact that he always picks a moment when my attention is momentarily distracted by a passing aroma of interest or the sudden need to inspect a tuft of carpet behind the easy chair or some such. The net result of this is that you waste a lot of time and effort trying to work out how the situation in the storyline has changed so dramatically before you finally realise that you're actually watching a completely different programme.

But what's really bewildering is when you're watching one of those foreign films on Channel Four. You look away for five minutes to give the old nether bits a quick wash, look back to discover that everything seems different and assume that he's changed channel again, then realise to your complete befuddlement that he hasn't. Honestly, these films are odd, I think they may show the reels in the wrong order, or maybe somebody dropped the script on the way to the studio and jumbled it all up. Or maybe they're just too subtle for us dogs to understand. But I doubt it.

I do like watching the commercials on the telly, it's probably the best bit of the programming. Not that the commercials themselves are much cop, mind you, but nonhuman species like Your Humble Author can grasp this opportunity to see how Mankind actually thinks, there being few other clues. It's also a way of seeing how Man views himself, and a pretty low opinion he's got if television advertising is anything to go by. I mean to say, are people really taken in by all that stuff?

I saw one the other day with a man who said that he only likes the best of everything and then plunged into a bag of crisps. Huh. If he only liked the good things in life how come he didn't sling the crisps in the bin and head for the nearest beefie?

Then there's one with a brace of stomachchurningly cute kittens rushing around and getting in everyone's way. And just when you think it must be a commercial for pest control or Preparation H, kittens being a pain in the...well, you know, it turns out to be selling toilet rolls, or bathroom stationery as the Boss is wont to call it in company. Typical feline ostentatiousness, of course. You wouldn't catch a dog being involved in anything quite so blatantly lavatorial.

You didn't know Labradors had a sense of irony, did you? I do have a soft spot for those dog food commercials, though, don't you? Lots of terribly well bred hounds looking frightfully grateful for a Bowlful of whatever it is, scoffing at full speed as if they were really enjoying it and yet it's the people in the commercial who get paid for the 'acting'

But telly really comes into its own for those events of National Importance, like Crufts. And then, of course, there's Election Night Special. Now I can already hear you asking yourself why someone as highminded as Your Humble Author should have even the mildest interest in something so utterly uninteresting and foolish as an election. Well, I'll tell you. Put politics quietly in your back pocket and try very hard not to refer to it at any stage. Regard, if you will, the behaviours of man in the electoral context rather than any numbers which may or may not be of interest to those people who seems to care about what's going on. Now read on.

As an involuntary Student of Mankind, I am particularly fond of Election Night Special because in our house it was an occasion of some note. Actually, it wasn't in our house at all we both went down to the Horse and Bookie where Stan Behind The Bar got a telly in specially and we all had a party. It was quite an exclusive party too, because as soon as the thing started to get going, Stan Behind The Bar locked the outside doors so that, presumably, gatecrashers couldn't come in late and spoil the atmosphere. And what an atmosphere! Riotous behaviour, cheers and boos, violent applause mingled with strangled cries of woe, intemperate language and drunken revelry with a side order of personal abuse and a light sprinkling of ostentatious overindulgence. Bit like 'Today in Parliament' really.

To the untrained eye, the whole exercise appeared no more or less than a handpicked selection of degenerate hooligans let loose in a gin palace, but the gifted psychologist, such as Your

Humble Parliamentary Correspondent, could very quickly identify Types and Patterns emerging from the mêlée.

For instance, there's the Working Class Hero expostulating on the way the rich look after their own and what about the workers and let's ban Capitalism and give Power back to the People and who's round is it and mine's a double brandy thank you very much, squire. And mind my Armani suit while you're pouring it, Stan.

Then there's the hard line Stick The Idle Buggers In The Army For A Spell Do Them A Power Of Good And A Sound Thrashing Never Did Me Any Harm Brigade, who consider Liberalism close to Satanic Worship and refuse to consider Socialism at all.

The majority seem to be the Well I Suppose It Would Be Nice If They're Weren't Any Poor People And Health And Education Should Be Free And I'm Sure The Russians Are The Same As Us Aren't They bunch, who don't really care which party gets in as long as they don't actually nuke anyone.

The Boss, as you might expect, falls very neatly into none of the foregoing categories, but belongs to a political force of his own called the 'I Strongly Agree With Whatever The Last Person Said' party. This makes political debate a little one sided, but the poor chap has always excelled at manning the periphery and really comes into his own when there's a Air of Indecision to be enhanced. He's a sort of professional Don't Know.

"Well, I don't know. I reckon I'll have another Ould Spleenburster, if that's alright with you." This was his strongest political statement of the entire evening, although I must admit it made far more sense to me than most of the drivel that was flying through the tobacco smoke near the bar.

Actually if you keep a firm eye on this sort of Event, you'll note that political loyalties tend to waver from side to side as the evening wears on and the level of Alcohol Ingested creeps from the Socially Acceptable to the Completely Ludicrous. Pick the right moment and you'll see arch enemies slap each other on the back or political allies on the very threshold of coming to blows over the precise meaning of the expression 'centrist devolutionary powerbase'

Punctuating all this uproar are the chaps on the telly, who really know what it's all about. These are: the Winners, who say 'this is a great victory and clearly shows that the country as a whole supports our policies'; the Losers, who say 'this is really a great victory and shows that the majority of the country taken as a whole does not support your policies'; the Commentators, who don't give a stuff what the country says as long as they can have a good laugh at the expense of the Losers. Mind you, it's a bit tricky to decipher what any of them is trying to say with all the racket being generated by the Politically Aware crashing into the furniture in an attempt to get to the bar.

By the time all the significant results were in, the Boss was starting to steer a fairly haphazard course himself, lurching from the relative security of the fireplace area, he likes to be near me in moments of crisis, to the loose maul that was working its way along the bar from the pistachio nut machine at one end to the lifeboat collection box at the other and back again.

Incidentally, have you ever wondered why pubs hundreds of miles inland find it appropriate to collect for the lifeboats? I can only assume that it's something to do with the comparable effects on the equilibrium of stormlashed seas and a couple of pints of Ould Spleenburster. As the average punter faces that increasing struggle with Gravity he can empathise with mariners going through the same confusion between horizontal and vertical and so hand over a dollop of loose change, almost as a talisman of protection against the common enemy of rolling decks and heaving waters. I have my own problems with Gravity, mind you, especially when bounding upstairs for an afternoon lie down. I have to sort of take it by surprise.

Anyway, the Election was hotting up to a Final Result, although to tell you the truth I had lost interest some time before when Stan Behind The Bar had run out of peanuts and the assembled masses were forced to nibble pork scratchings. I hate pork scratchings and risked giving offence for the future by growling darkly whenever a fistful of these awful things was thrust in my direction.

I suppose I need not have worried, though. From the condition of His Lordship the next morning, I imagine my fellow Electionists of the previous evening would have had difficulty bringing their own names to mind, let alone remembered that their Favourite Peanut Nosher had shown such deplorable ingratitude.

This sorrowful state of his lasted right through to lunchtime, when he decided that a small pint of Ould Spleenburster was the only possible cure for the severe case of partial death that he was suffering. We strolled, very slowly, in the general direction of the Horse and Bookie, where we were met with a scene reminiscent of a First World War Dressing Station. Lines of men mooched around the place, each with a hand on the shoulder of the one in front. Everywhere there were moans and groans. Stan Behind The Bar had the look of a man who has glanced through the Gates of Hell and spotted his mother in law in charge.

The pub itself did not exactly look as though a bomb had hit it, but looked as though it ought to. The carpets had taken on the hue of crushed peanuts and crisps, with a thin veneer of fag ash. There was a sort of damp, fruity smell in the air, like an orchard full of rotten apples after rain. The whole scene had a deathly pallor like a mortuary on a bad day, thrown into sharper relief by the memory of the bright lights and raucous fun of the night before. Armageddon, I thought to myself, will be like this; three notches to the depressing side of bland.

I wormed my way through the shattered landscape of misplaced tables and chairs and took up Position A by the fire, which was unlit and full of ashes mixed with empty fag packets, bits of beer mat and what appeared at first sight to be a set of dentures but turned out to be part of the scalloped hem of the curtains. The floor seemed to have grown lumpy overnight and I found it impossible to get comfy, so I decided to abandon all hope of a quiet snooze and wandered back over for the pleasure of watching the Boss in his alimentary torment. He had taken his first tentative pulls at the Ould Spleenburster,

and some colour had returned to his cheeks. Unfortunately the returning colour was green.

Have you ever had one of those days when you simply don't know where to put yourself? I felt out of place in amongst all this agony, as the only non participant and hence the sole creature present with all the brain cells in line and facing forwards. I don't know what you chaps do to yourselves in the pursuit of having a good time. It completely defeats me.

Chapter 10 A Muse on a Winter's Afternoon

As I survey the world through the little holes formed by the wickerwork of my basket, it occurs to me that Life probably is just a bowl of cherries. And what's more, there's a good fistful or two of mouldy ones. Still, consider the alternative.

But it's difficult, not to say churlish, to be too critical about Life when you're snugly curled up with a tummy full of recent repast and a full set of Direct Sell Double Glazing between you and the Cold Outdoors. And there's something very comforting about the crackle and the dancing light of a log fire at fever pitch, especially when it spits bits out and sends the Boss scurrying over wielding a pair of fire tongs.

Life, eh? That rocky journey from your first Biorhythmical Triple Critical to your last sad wag of a limp appendage. That ill considered trifle that someone forgot to put the sherry in. That Sacred Gift which wasn't quite what you wanted for Christmas but you put a brave face on it in case you're seen to be ungrateful.

Life. What's it all about, eh? Well, I'll tell you. It's about small triumphs and small disasters and the trick is to make sure you have more of the former than the latter. It's also about putting all your energies into having to do as little as possible. For the professional, idleness is a fulltime job. Some of the best creative ideas in history started by someone trying to find an easier way to do something, so you can ignore out of hand all that rubbish about nothing being worthwhile unless you have to struggle for it that Camus was so fond of. Actually I won't hear a word against Camus after discovering the chap he wrote about who was wont to spit at cats. Sensible sort of homme, if you ask me.

Look at all the marvellous Technology there is around the place nowadays. You can get feed bowls for cats with a built in timer so that the obnoxious beasts can't munch their way through a whole day's allocation in one go. Frankly, the more of these devices that break down, the happier I'll be, but it goes to show that technology has become so commonplace that they even use it on cats.

And there are those wonderful extending leads for dogs you see around the park. I'm so pleased I haven't got one. A lead that long is something and nothing as far as I'm concerned; too long for you to control the bod at the other end and too short for a really good unaccompanied rummage in the undergrowth. I favour the short leather and chain jobs; you can raise smashing weals on the Boss's hand with a protracted tug on one of those. And it looks so fetching with the matching collar.

Mind you, technology has found a place in the human experience too. Take those DVD jobs. Wonderful idea. Now you can fall asleep in the evening during the same programme you fell asleep during in the afternoon. And then there's the MP3 player which allows the user to shut out the rest of the world while he floats on a sea of music brought directly to his ears. Unfortunately there's no device yet for the rest of the world to shut him and his stupid music out.

Have you seen these radio controlled boats like the ones they use in the ornamental lake near the playground? These things whiz round and round frightening the ducks and making an intensely irritating high pitched buzzing noise. They go nowhere. They have no purpose. They are very expensive. No, I don't understand it either.

Still, technology is a wonderful thing. Man has strolled on the moon, wiped out two or three diseases, gained power from splitting the atom, discovered the secret of life from the DNA double helix and learned to fly at three times the speed of sound. And invented radio controlled model boats. Marvellous, isn't it?

With Technology sprinting headlong into the Twenty First Century it may well be that he will discover ways of rounding up sheep, sniffing out drugs and explosives and tracking fugitives. At the moment, such simple tasks are quite beyond the poor chap, but maybe, one day, he'll get the hang of it.

Now that's a dangerous job, sniffing out naughty substances. Suppose you get a taste for it, eh? Where is your average hound going to find a reliable source for a puff or two of the old Head Rearranger? I can't see knots of police dogs hanging around on street corners waiting for the Man to come along with a batch of goodies, can you? Doesn't seem fair, somehow.

And then there's the poor beggars that have to wade through mud or scamper through thistles to retrieve the riddled remains of some unsuspecting pheasant that only moments before was wandering through the sky minding its own business before being rudely interrupted by half a ton of lead shot. This is an intolerable intrusion. If they're so keen on blowing passing livestock to bits just for the fun of it, let them go and pick up the corpses themselves, that's what I say.

Anyway, I don't like pheasant; a bit too gamey for my taste and I get fed up having to keep spitting out bits of buckshot. Why don't they do something really useful and invent radio controlled pheasants? Then they could blast them out of the sky and twiddle a few knobs to make the carcase retrieve itself, so saving everyone concerned a lot of time and trouble. Perhaps they could build in some form of random programme so that this mass aerial slaughter is not quite so inevitable. Or maybe they could fix it so that the pheasants could shoot back and make things really interesting.

Actually, musing on Technology always reminds me of the Day the Boss bought a new washing machine, one of those newfangled jobs with programmes for heavy soil whites, an expression which conjures up some rather unpleasant images if you ask me. Anyway, the thing arrived on the back of the van and was manhandled to the front door by two gentlemen whose name appeared to be Fred.

As the kitchen is at the back of the house, it meant that the brace of Freds had to steer the thing around an obstacle course formed by various items of furniture.

Now I don't know how much this sort of thing weighs, but the Freds seem to be making unnecessarily heavy weather of it. First they bashed into the doorway leading into the sitting room, then they took the stretch cover neatly off the sofa before kicking over the occasional table and heading at full speed into one of the unmatched pair of armchairs.

The next port of call was the sideboardy sort of thing where the Boss keeps his semi collection of ceramic thimbles celebrating the works of Christopher Marlowe. He had actually intended to order a kimono style robe but had filled in and sent

off the wrong coupon in the Sunday supplement. Total inertia
had then prevented him sending them back.

As the washing machine met the sideboard, Tamburlaine
the Great leapt into the fireplace and Doctor Faustus nosedived
into the log basket. Barabas, the Jew of Malta, tottered for a
while then fell backwards into Helen of Troy, knocking her
onto Edward the Second who rolled off the side and onto the
hard edge of the doorstep into the kitchen. There were no
survivors.

The Freds finally managed to heave the machine into the
kitchen and over to the space that the Boss had carefully
prepared for it, mostly by moving out the old one. Technology
being what it is, the new machine was considerably shorter
than its predecessor, but slightly wider. This left a huge dust
collect potential at the top and a deep scratch along the side as
the two worthies used full power to squeeze the delicate
machinery into the slot, rather like the Boss trying to get into a
pair of old moleskin trousers four sizes too small. They then
squeezed the machine out of the slot when the Boss pointed

out, and quite reasonably too I thought, that all the gubbins for connecting the thing were at the back.

There was a sort of mutual feeling of despair at this, so they all had a cup of tea and a fag while they mused over the problem in hand. The obvious answer was to connect the thing, then slide it gently into the gap, but it took their combined intellect and a second cup of tea before this staggering truth occurred to them.

"Ah," said the Boss by way of introduction, "why don't we connect it up first, then slide it into the gap. Are the pipes long enough?" They were. Just. So in she went, gently, at a slightly different angle than before, giving Freds the opportunity to add a second scratch to match the first. Such an eye for detail. By and by there was a washing machine. Then there was another cup of tea. Then the Freds said 'Right, see you then, Guv'nor' a lot. Then they left.

Now when it comes to Great Art, I'm afraid I rank the washing machine some way behind Giotto or Mantegna. It doesn't have the emotion of a Van Gogh or the studied perspective of a Uccello. As a piece of sculpture, it's not a patch on Michelangelo or Moore. And yet the Boss stood, transfixed, before his new toy as though it was La Gioconde and he Da Vinci. He studied every angle. He ran his fingers lightly over the control panel. He stooped to gaze lovingly into the little window at the front. I began to suspect insanity.

After a while he disappeared upstairs, to reemerge bearing a large writhing mass of socks, pants, shirts, vests, hankies and one or two other items that I couldn't immediately identify but which I bet were those heavy soil whites. He stuffed this assortment into the hole at the front, the one behind the window, and switched on the machine. At this, the control panel leapt into illuminated life and took on the look of the dashboard of a space ship. Some lights were green, some orange, others yellow. One was red. It all looked rather pretty; perhaps I was wrong about its artistic worth.

I sat back in sneaking admiration as the Boss pressed buttons, whirled knobs and lifted levers with the air of a man who knows what he's doing. He didn't, of course. We were halfway through a concerto of rushing water, clicks and dunks when he spotted the fact that he had neglected to put in any washing powder. I'd already noticed this oversight, but forbore to mention it because a) I wanted to see what would happen and b) such a complicated message would be impossible for him to comprehend in fluent Labrador.

From what I could see, there was no way of stopping the machine once it had made up its mind. The Boss frantically scoured the instruction manual for the Answer, but the bit he was looking at was all in Swedish and his grasp of foreign languages comes to a shuddering halt well this side of Dover. Meanwhile, the selection of nonspecific articles of wear were ploshing about for all they were worth in the steadfastly unsoapy water. But the keen observer, such as Your H A, could see through the window that a strange metamorphosis was taking place. As the apparel lounged wetly this way and that, rising and falling with the motion of the water, I could see that the water was not only getting dirty, it was also getting blue. I mean, really blue, not the blue of the Mediterranean around Crete but the blue of, well, blue water. I felt this might be a mistake. I nudged the Boss lightly above the knee and glared hard at the window.

"No, old chap," he said, for no reason that I can think of. I decided to let him get on with it, after all, it wasn't my problem and he won't be told, you know.

After what seemed like a weekend in Redditch the machine uttered a final click and stopped. The little lights went out and we were suddenly bathed in an exhausted silence. Gingerly, the Master Technician reached out and pressed a button. The door opened.

Inside was an entire collection of matching, marbled, light blue clothing. No more heavy soil whites but a whole range of heavy soil light blues. I feared that some error had been made here, a conclusion reinforced by the look of horror that sprinted across the bland countenance immediately above me and to the right. Oh dear. All this because of a misplaced pair of denim jeans. I'm sure this sort of thing didn't happen when they did their washing on a stone by the river.

But enough of wash day wittering and back to me and my muse. I suppose I have quite a good lifestyle, really. I mean, I don't have my own place or a fast car, and I don't nip off to Juan les Pins for the season or Gstaad for the skiing or anything, but there's more to life than travel and transport. There's beefburgers, for example.

And there's peace of mind. That means knowing where your next meal is coming from, if not necessarily knowing when or what. It means a comfortable billet with a flunkey who would gratify your slightest whim if only he knew what it was. It means being content with what you have and not worrying about what the dog over the fence has got. In my case, the dog over the fence has got hardpad, but that's another story.

And it means having your health. Now I'm not one of these dogs that takes to the Basket whenever they get the odd sniffle, in fact, I don't remember having a day's illness in my life. Good, hardy stock, we Labradors, unlike some of those poor little lap dogs who look permanently anaemic.

I met a Chihuahua once called Petal, and yet for some reason he never bit his Lady and Mistress once. Marvellous self control. If anyone had named me Petal, I'd have made damned sure that Saint Peter at the Pearly Gates got to hear about it fairly quickly from the person concerned. Anyway, the poor little chap was forever coughing and sneezing. And the more he coughed and sneezed, the more his Bossess clutched him to her enormous furlined bosom, with the net result that he was part suffocated, part roasted and almost completely engulfed. If you watched closely, you could see a grossly embarrassed Chihuahua glancing out at the world from time to time.

Now he had one of those tartan coats, well, it was more of a straitjacket really. He was never allowed to larrup in the park or lunge into the nearest thicket, copse or spinney for a game of Hunt The Smell I Can't At First Sniff Identify, But I Think

It Comes From Around This Extremely Muddy Bit Somewhere. He was utterly spoiled and utterly miserable. Never had a beefburger off a plate in his life. What kind of existence is that for a dog?

No, I'm proud of my good health. Regular visits to the vet (but I do wish he'd find some other way of taking my temperature), plenty of carefully selected exercise, good varied diet, that's all it takes. I have a nose that glistens and a coat so glossy it dazzles Traffic Wardens in the street.

It's a pity the Boss isn't the ostentatious type, or all those so called Supreme Champions at Crufts would be up against it, I can tell you. Still, who needs public adulation to prove what you already know, viz. when it comes to the Champion of Champions, I just happen to know his address and phone number.

I've got it written on my collar.

#0153 - 301116 - C0 - 210/148/6 - PB - DID1673778